Restoration in the Church

Restoration in the Church

Reports of Revivals
1625–1839

with a foreword by J. Douglas MacMillan

Christian Focus Publications Ltd

Published in Northern Ireland by Ambassador Productions Ltd

First published in 1839 under the title Narratives of Revivals
of Religion in Scotland, Ireland and Wales.

Published under the superintendence of the
Glasgow Revival Tract Society

This edition published by
Christian Focus Publications Ltd
Houston   **Tain**
Texas   **Ross-shire**

© 1989 Christian Focus Publications Ltd

ISBN 0 871676 02 9

Published in Northern Ireland by
Ambassador Productions Ltd
16 Hillview Avenue
Belfast
BT5 6JR

ISBN 0 907927 46 7

Printed in Great Britain by
Billing & Sons Ltd, Worcester

Restoration in the Church

Contents

Foreword

Living in the closing years of the Twentieth century it is hard for us to imagine what a time of true, heaven-sent, spiritual awakening would be like. Most of us have experienced times of Gospel power that produce packed churches, powerful preaching, convicted sinners and crowds of new converts to Christ. Yet such times characterise the Christian era. Church history speaks of them as 'Times of Revival', the bible as 'Times of refreshing from the presence of the Lord.' Whenever they have occurred they have radically affected not only individuals but entire communities, and even society at large. This is the sort of visitation our land and our churches urgently need today but it is one of which, in practical terms, we know nothing at all.

This is not because God has deserted the world, or the Gospel has lost anything of its truth or its power. In fact, the opposite is true. Although our land has not been visited with Revival, this century has seen sweeping movements of the Spirit of God in many other lands. The Church in Asia and in Africa has seen great advances made in the work of the Gospel with millions of people coming under its power. In fact, these movements have been such that the last hundred years show the greatest period of growth for the Christian faith, worldwide, since New Testament times. Until very recently, however, this phenomenal advance, and the spiritual awakenings of its heart, have gone almost unnoticed by people in the West.

But if our generation has not known Revival, this was not always the case in these Islands of ours. The great Reformation Movements of the Sixteenth century, which transformed the lives of our forefathers, shaped our country's history, and took our churches back to the simplicities and spiritual realities of New Testament Christianity, had Revival at their centre and core. Not only so, but each century from then until our own has known times of refreshing and awakening that have renewed the Church and transformed the lives of countless multitudes. It is of such times as those that this little book which you have in your hands speaks.

The work brings before us, in a simple but attractive fashion, contemporary accounts of Revival in times as far apart as 1623 and 1839, the year in which it was first published. The stories take us to Wales and across the sea to Ireland, and show us God at work among different people and in different circumstances. No effort is made to link the narratives, but none is required. The awakenings span time and place, linking spiritual realities, with their variations in detail, into the work of the one Spirit and the effects of the same truths — the truths of God's Work. Yet, the variety of style and the complete lack of striving for effect makes the work, in its movement through different times and places, easy and pleasant to read.

For the Christian reader, the events recounted make a gripping and moving story. It tells of the men, the circumstances, the churches, the communities on whom the Spirit of God came down in sudden, and sometimes unexpected, seasons of spiritual power. The stories have their individual features and, naturally enough, emphases differ in the hands of the different authors, but all convey the same cheerful — often cautious — accounts of the work and the results it left behind in the lives of multitudes of ordinary people.

Like the Book of Acts, the stories speak to us of how the Lord, when He pleases, can and does prosper the work of the Gospel and bless the preaching of His Word in an unusual way. The mighty power of God's grace, coming in swift, sovereign, conviction to the most hardened sinners and the most ungodly of men as well as the formal religionist and the nominal Christian, is the common factor in all the narratives. The great, basic truths of the Gospel — Ruin by the Fall, Redemption through Christ, Regeneration through the Spirit and Righteousness through faith — became, at such times, the specific themes of the pulpit and through them, God laid hold of men, women and even children, blessing them with lasting effect. Those stories of Revival vividly demonstrate what Scripture everywhere teaches, that true conversion to Christ flows only out of a renewing work of the Spirit in the hearts of people who, by nature, are 'dead in trepasses and sin' — and that is a truth the Evangelical Church of today needs to relearn very urgently. This book teaches it in a memorable way.

I wish to thank the present Publishers for making it available to us again and for extending to me the privilege of writing this short Foreword by way of explanation and commendation of its content and worth. I regard this as a very pleasant task indeed and I am not only happy, but anxious, to commend the work to all into whose hands it comes. It will richly repay everyone who takes it up to read and the more carefully it is read and studied then the more useful, I believe, it will prove. My desire for what it may achieve is well expressed by those who first put the volume into circulation and so I reiterate their words: 'The work of which it treats attracted the attention, and greatly rejoiced the hearts of Christians at the time, and it may, through the divine blessing, encourage the hopes and stimulate the prayers of Christians at the present day.'

J. Douglas MacMillan
The Free Church College
Edinburgh.
February 1989.

REVIVALS OF RELIGION.

No. I.

CAMBUSLANG, 1742.

EVERY Christian is aware of the descent of the Holy Spirit on the day of Pentecost, and the amazing success which accompanied the preaching of the gospel immediately thereafter; but very many are ignorant that God has since, from time to time, refreshed his heritage, and extended the kingdom of his Son, in a manner almost equally remarkable. This ignorance induces a belief that Zion is to be enlarged only in the silent and gradual manner of our own day: and it is to be feared that Christians, in pleading for the outpouring of the Holy Ghost, have so little expectation of obtaining their request, that they would be astonished beyond measure were their prayers answered. They pray for the outpouring of the Spirit because the word of God teaches them to do so, and yet they are hopeless of succeeding in their suit, although the same word engages that the prayer of faith shall not be in vain. The inconsistency is striking, and it is melancholy; for so long as it obtains, we cannot look for those displays of divine power in the conversion of sinners, which we might otherwise warrantably anticipate. As a means of leading to a better state of mind, it is well to be acquainted with what God has already done in answer to prayer; and that we may the more readily expect the fulfilment of what he has engaged yet to do, the following narrative has been drawn up. The work of which it treats attracted the attention and greatly rejoiced the hearts of Christians at the time, and it may, through the divine blessing, encourage the hopes and stimulate the prayers of Christians at the present day.

Cambuslang is a parish about four miles south-east of Glasgow, and, at the time of this revival, was under the

pastoral care of Mr. M'CULLOCH, a man of decided piety
and anxiously desirous of the spiritual welfare of his people. In his ordinary course of sermons for nearly a year
before the work began, he had been preaching on those subjects which tend most directly to explain the nature and
prove the necessity of regeneration; and for some months
before the remarkable events now about to be mentioned,
a more then ordinary concern about religion appeared
among his flock; as an evidence of which, a petition was
given in to him, subscribed by about ninety heads of families, desiring a weekly lecture, which was readily granted.
This was in the beginning of February, 1742. On the
15th of that month, the different prayer meetings in the
parish assembled at his house, and next day they again met
for solemn prayer, relative to the interests of the gospel.
Although this second meeting was of a more private description, others getting notice of it, desired to join, and
were admitted: and on the day following they met a third
time for the same purpose. At this period, though several
persons had come to the minister under deep concern
about their salvation, there had been no great number;
but on Thursday the 18th, after sermon, about fifty came
to him under alarming apprehensions about the state of
their souls; and such was their anxiety, that he had to pass
the night in conversing with them.

After this, the desire of the people for religious instruction was so great, that Mr. M'Culloch found himself
obliged to provide them a sermon almost daily; and after
sermon, he had generally to spend some time with them in
exhortation and prayer: and the blessing of God on these
ordinances was so great, that by the beginning of May,
the number of persons awakened to a deep concern about
salvation exceeded three hundred.

About this time, (June, 1742,) Mr. Whitefield revisited
Scotland, and in consequence of earnest invitations, he
came to the west country, and to Cambuslang amongst
other places, where, with his customary zeal, he preached
three times on the very day of his arrival, to a vast body
of people, although he had preached the same morning at
Glasgow. The last of these exercises began at nine in the
evening, and continued till eleven; and such was the relish for the word of life, that Mr. M'Culloch preached after
him till past one in the morning, and even then the people

could hardly be persuaded to depart. All night, in the fields, the voice of prayer and praise was to be heard.

The sacrament of the supper was dispensed on the 11th of July, and the solemnity was so remarkably blessed that it was speedily repeated. The following extract of a letter written by Mr. M'Culloch, giving an account of the proceedings at this period, will be read with interest:—

"The dispensation of the sacrament was such a sweet and agreeable time to many, that a motion was made by Mr. Webster, and immediately seconded by Mr. Whitefield, that we should have another such occasion in this place very soon. The motion was very agreeable to me, but I thought it needful to deliberate before coming to a resolution. The thing proposed was extraordinary, but so had the work been for several months. Care was therefore taken to acquaint the several meetings for prayer, who relished the motion well, and prayed for direction to those concerned to determine this matter. The session met next Lord's day, and taking into consideration the divine command to celebrate the ordinance often, joined with the extraordinary work that had been here for some time past; and understanding that many who had met with much benefit to their souls at the last solemnity, had expressed an earnest desire of seeing another in this place shortly; and hearing that there were many who intended to have joined at the last occasion, but were kept back through inward discouragements, or outward obstructions, and were wishing soon to see another opportunity of that kind here, to which they might have access;—it was therefore resolved, God willing, that the sacrament of the Lord's Supper should be again dispensed in this parish, on the third Sabbath of August: and there was first one day, and then another, appointed for a general meeting of the several societies for prayer in the parish, at the manse; but as the manse could not conveniently hold them, they went to the church, and when light failed them there, a good many, of their own free motion, returned to the manse, and continued at prayer and praise till about one o'clock next morning. One design of these meetings was, to ask that the Lord would continue and increase the blessed work of conviction and conversion, and eminently countenance the dispensing of the holy sacrament of the supper a second time in this place, and thereby make the glory of this latter solemnity to exceed that of the former.

"This second sacrament did, indeed, much excel the former, not only in the number of ministers, people, and communicants, but, which is the main thing, in a much greater measure of the power and special presence of God, in the observation and experie?ce of multitudes who were attending.

"The ministers who assisted at this solemnity, were Mr. Whitefield, Mr. Webster from Edinburgh, Mr. M'Laurin and Mr. Gillies from Glasgow, Mr. Robe from Kilsyth, Mr. Currie from Kinglassie, Mr. M'Kneight from Irvine, Mr. Bonner from Torphichen, Mr. Hamilton from Douglas, Mr. Henderson from Blantyre, Mr. Maxwell from Rutherglen, and Mr. Adam from Cathcart. All of them appeared to be very much assisted in their work. Four of them preached on the fast day; four on Saturday; on Sabbath I cannot well tell how many; and five on Monday; on which last day it was computed that above twenty-four ministers and preachers were present. Old Mr. Bonner, though so frail that he took three days to ride eighteen miles from Torphichen to Cambuslang, was so set upon coming here, that he could by no means stay away; and when he was helped up to the tent, preached three times with great life; and returned with much satisfaction and joy. Mr. Whitefield's sermons on Saturday and Sabbath were attended with much power, particularly on Sabbath night about ten, and that on Monday, several crying out, and a very great but devout weeping and mourning was observable through the auditory. On Sabbath evening, while he was serving some tables, he appeared to be so filled with the love of God, as to be in a kind of ecstacy or transport, and communicated with much of that blessed frame.

"The number of people that were there on Saturday and Monday was very considerable: but the number present, at the three tents, on the Lord's day, was so great, that, so far as I can hear, none ever saw the like since the Revolution in Scotland; nor even anywhere else, at any sacrament occasion: some have called them fifty thousand —some forty thousand. The lowest estimate I hear of, with which Mr. Whitefield agrees, who has been much used to great multitudes, makes them to have been upwards of thirty thousand.

"The number of communicants appears to have been

about three thousand. The tables were doubled, and the double table was reckoned to contain one hundred and fourteen, one hundred and sixteen, or one hundred and twenty communicants. The number of tables I reckoned had been about twenty-four, but I have been since informed, that a man who sat near the tables, and kept a pen in his hand, and carefully marked each service, said that there were twenty-five double tables, the last wanting only five or six sitters to fill it up. And this account seems the most probable, as agreeing nearly with the number of tokens distributed, which was about three thousand. And some worthy of credit, and that had proper opportunities to know, gave it as their opinion, that there was such a blessed frame upon the people, that if there had been access to tokens, there would have been a thousand more communicants.

"This vast concourse of people, you may easily imagine, came not only from the city of Glasgow and other places near by, but from many places at a considerable distance. It was reckoned there were two hundred communicants from Edinburgh, two hundred from Kilmarnock, one hundred from Irvine, and one hundred from Stewarton. It was observed that there were some from England and Ireland at this occasion; a considerable number of Quakers were hearers, and some that had formerly been Seceders were communicants.

"There was a great deal of outward decency and regularity about the tables. Public worship began on the Lord's day just at half-past eight in the morning. My action sermon, I think, was reasonably short. The third or fourth table was a-serving at twelve o'clock, and the last table about sunset. When that was done, the work was closed with a few words of exhortation, prayer, and praise, the precentor having so much daylight as to let him read four lines of a psalm. The passes to and from the tables were, with great care, kept clear for the communicants. The tables filled so quickly, that often there was no more time between one table and another, then to sing four lines of a psalm. The tables were all served in the open air, beside the tent below the brae; the day was temperate; no rain nor wind in the least to disturb. Several persons of considerable rank and distinction, who were elders, most cheerfully assisted our elders in serving tables; such as the honourable Charles Erskine Bruce of Kennet, Gillon of Wallhouse, and others.

"But what was most remarkable, was the spiritual glory of this solemnity; I mean the gracious and sensible presence of God. Not a few were awakened to a sense of sin, and their lost and perishing condition without a Saviour. Others had their bands loosed, and were brought into the glorious liberty of the sons of God. Many of God's dear children have declared, that it was a happy time to their souls, wherein they were abundantly satisfied with the goodness of God in his ordinances, and filléd with joy and peace in believing. I have seen a letter from Edinburgh, the writer of which says, that having talked with many Christians from that city, who had been here at this sacrament, they all owned that God had dealt bountifully with their souls. Some declared that they would not for the world have been absent from this solemnity. Others cried out, 'Now let thy servants depart in peace from this place, since our eyes have seen thy salvation here.' Others wishing, if it were the will of God, to die where they were, attending God in his ordinances, without returning to the world or their friends, that they might be with Christ in heaven, as that which is incomparably best of all."

Such is the substance of Mr. M'Culloch's account of this remarkable period; and as Mr. Whitefield was frequently at Cambuslang about this time, the following observations, given nearly in his own words, will be interesting. "Persons from all parts flocked to see, and many from many parts went home convinced and converted unto God. A brae, or hill, near the manse at Cambuslang, seemed to be formed by Providence for containing a large congregation. People sat unwearied till two in the morning to hear sermons, disregarding the weather. You could scarce walk a yard but you must tread upon some, either rejoicing in God for mercies received, or crying out for more. Thousands and thousands have I seen, before it was possible to catch it by sympathy, melted down under the word and power of God. At the celebration of the holy communion, their joy was so great, that, at the desire of many, both ministers and people, in imitation of Hezekiah's passover, they had, a month or two afterwards, a second, which was a general rendezvous for the people of God. The communion-table was in the field; three tents at proper distances, all surrounded by a multitude of hearers; above twenty ministers (among whom was good old Mr. Bonner) attending to preach and assist, all enlivening and enlivened by one another."

Amongst the multitudes that flocked to Cambuslang at this interesting period, there were persons who went with a design to find matter of diversion; and while the bands of such mockers were, no doubt, generally made stronger, others were made happy monuments of divine grace. The case of two young men may be mentioned, as affording a striking example of sovereign mercy. They were very profane, and had gone over to be amused with "the falling" at Cambuslang, as they jestingly termed it; but in place of being amused, they were both impressed the same day; and so deep were their convictions, that they were glad to get into a stable hard by, for the purpose of supplicating that grace which they had hitherto despised, and their subsequent conduct afforded reason to conclude, that the word they had that day heard had proved the savour of life to their souls.

As to what these young men termed "the falling," it was a way of speaking among scoffers at the time, occasioned by the bodily distress which, in many instances, accompanied conviction. The work was much objected to in consequence; but when the intimate connection of soul and body is considered, it will not appear surprising that great outward agitation should mark the emotions of a soul fully awakened to the dread realities of judgment and eternity. The loss of a dear relative, and many of the other painful vicissitudes of life, when suddenly forced upon the mind, affect the bodily constitution so powerfully as, in some instances, to occasion even death. And if such is sometimes the effect of things merely temporal, need we wonder that a vivid sense of the sinner's situation out of Christ, with nothing but the brittle thread of life between him and everlasting destruction, should overpower the body! The wonder rather is, that the preaching of the solemn truths of God's word is so rarely followed by such consequences; and we can account for this only by supposing, that the Spirit of God does not make the sinner at once alive to all the terrors of his condition. With regard to the revival at Cambuslang, the greater number of the subjects of it were not observably under bodily distress and as for those who were, their lives proved that they had been made partakers of divine grace: which is a proof that such agitation is, at least, not inconsistent with a work of the Holy Ghost.

The narrative now given has been fully attested by the most able and pious ministers of the time, and their attestations might be transcribed here did space permit. Amongst others who have borne testimony to this glorious display of divine power, are Mr. M'Laurin, of the Northwest Church of Glasgow, (now St. David's,) well known by his remarkable sermon on the Cross of Christ; Mr. Hamilton, of the Barony Parish; Mr. Hamilton, of Bothwell; Mr. Hamilton, of Douglas; and Mr. Connell, of Kilbride. Mr. Willison, of Dundee, also, has recorded his opinion, and the following extract shows what were his sentiments:—"Seeing some are desirous to know my thoughts of the work at Cambuslang, I am willing to own that I have travelled a good way to inquire and get satisfaction about it. And having resided several days in Mr. M'Culloch's house, I had occasion to converse with many who had been awakened and under convictions there; I found severals in darkness and great distress about their souls' condition, and with many tears bewailing their sins and original corruption, and especially the sin of unbelief, and slighting of precious Christ. Others I found in a most desirable frame, overcome with a sense of the wonderful love and loveliness of Jesus Christ, *even sick of love*, and inviting all about them to help them to praise him. I spoke also with many who had got relief from their soul trouble, and in whom the gracious work of the Spirit of God appeared in the fruits and effects of it, according to my apprehension; such as their ingenuous confessing of their former evil ways, and professing a hatred to sin; very low and abasing thoughts of themselves; renouncing the vanities of the world, and all their own doings and righteousness, and relying wholly upon Christ for righteousness and strength: and expressing great love to Christ, to the Bible, to secret prayer, to the people of God, and to his image, in whomsoever it was, without respect of persons or parties; and also love to their enemies. I conversed with some who had been very wicked and scandalous, but now wonderfully changed; though some were rude and boisterous before, they now had the meekness and mildness of the lamb about them, and though I conversed with a great number, both men and women, old and young, I could observe nothing visionary or enthusiastic about them, for their discourses were solid, and experiences scriptural; I had heard much of this surprising work by letters, and by eye-witnesses, before I came, but all that made slight impressions on me when compared with what I was eye- and ear-witness to myself. Upon the whole, I look upon the work at Cambuslang, to be a most singular and marvelous outpouring of the Holy Spirit, which Christ hath promised; and I pray it may be a happy forerunner of a general reviving of the work of God in this poor decayed Church, and a blessed mean of union among all the lovers of our dear Jesus."

We have likewise the testimony of Mr. M'Culloch himself, who, in a letter written about nine years after the revival, and when ample time had been afforded to test the sincerity of the professions then made, writes nearly as follows:—"Setting aside all those that appeared under awakenings here in 1742, who have since remarkably backslidden, there is a considerable number of the then awakened that appear to bring forth good fruits. I do not talk of them at random, nor speak of their number in a loose, general, and confused way, but have now before me, at the writing of this, April 27th, 1751, a list of about four hundred persons awakened here, at Cumbuslang, in 1742, who from that time to the time of their death, or to this, that is, for these nine years past, have been all enabled to behave, in a good measure, as becometh the gospel, by any thing I could ever see, and by the best information I could get concerning them." While this letter furnishes such satisfactory evidence of the reality of the work, the following paragraph, from the same communication, affords a beautiful proof of the humility of him who was a main instrument in promoting it. "When I mention such comfortable abiding effects of this work, I would not have it ascribed to any creature, but that the entire glory of it should be given to God, whose work it was. It is true, there were many ministers here, from places near and more remote; and some of them men of great eminence, who preached here at my desire, and who also joined with me in exhortation to souls appearing in spiritual distress, who resorted to the manse. But what could all these avail without the divine power and blessing? Whoever plant and water, it is God that gives the increase. Ministers are but instruments in his hands. No praise was due to the rams' horns, though Jericho's walls fell down at their blast: if God will vouchsafe that his word shall breathe through ministers, it is God, and not the means, must have the praise. It is very fit and reasonable that he that builds the temple should bear the glory: and Christ is both the foundation and founder of the Church, and therefore let all the glory be ascribed to him."

The period which elapsed between 1740 and 1750, forms an important era in the religious history, not of the little village of Cambuslang only, but it may almost be said of Scotland, as revivals were then very general. During these ten years a great multitude of souls were added to the Church; and it is important to remark, that a spirit of prayer was extensively prevalent. In illustration of this, the substance of a letter, written at Edinburgh in 1743, by Mr. George Muir, afterwards one of the ministers of Paisley, may be quoted:—

"The praying societies in this place are, as near as we can guess, between twenty-four and thirty; some of which will be obliged to divide, by reason of too many meeting together, which will increase the number. Amongst them are several meetings of boys and girls, who, in general, seem to be growing in grace, and increasing in knowledge. The little lambs appear to be unwilling to rest upon duties, or any thing short of Christ. There are several meetings of young women, who, I am informed, hold on very well; and there are numbers of young men, who meet for the excellent purpose of glorifying God, and promoting Christian knowledge. A good many old men, substantial, standing Christians, meet for edification, (the glory of their God being always their chief end,) and are thereby often revived and very much refreshed. This is not all; for several country people are beginning to assemble together, in little meetings, to worship God; and I am informed, that, about two miles from this place, several ploughmen, and other illiterate persons, meet, and are going sweetly on, having some added to their number daily. In the east country, also, near Dunbar, many are now meeting for social prayer and conversation upon religious matters, having the Lord with them of a truth; and in that place, there is a more eager thirsting for the word, and the ministers are learning to speak with new tongues."

Such remarkable manifestations of the Holy Spirit have been so long withheld from the churches of Scotland, that many who bear the name of Christian are tempted to think, that his affecting operations on the souls of men, through the preaching of the gospel, belonged only to the extraordinary ministrations of the apostles; and that now no more is necessary, in order to make men good Christians, but a mere rational conviction of the deformity of vice, and of the beauty and excellency of virtue. An external profession of religion, with a general assent to the truths of revelation, and a life unblameable in the eye of human laws, are all that is considered needful, though, at the same time, the person be an absolute stranger to the faith of God's elect, and to the indwelling of the Spirit of Christ, having made no particular application of Jesus Christ to himself, nor having been brought to rest upon him alone for the whole of his salvation; and yet it is as certain as God's word is true, that unless the most moral man in the world is " born again, he cannot enter into the kingdom of God;" and that " if any man have not the Spirit of Christ," be he otherwise what he will, " he is none of his." Great, and, alas! too successful endeavours have been made to bring men to rest upon a ministry and ordinances without the Spirit.

By nature we love not God, nor the things of God. The Sabbath is a weariness—the Scriptures are without interest, and the ordinances of God's house possess no attraction. In this state we are obviously unfit for the eternal Sabbath, and for the blessed employments of the upper sanctuary. We must be changed if we would ever enjoy these. This change the Spirit of God accomplishes on every soul that comes to Christ. Our tastes, therefore, afford a plain test by which our state may be ascertained. Reader, have *you* any relish for these things? Have *you* any sympathy with the hungering and thirsting after God which was so remarkably displayed at Cambuslang? If you have not—if conscience tells you that religion is unsavoury—it is certain that you are without Christ, and consequently without hope. Up then, and flee to Christ: delay not, for " now is the accepted time." The needful change the Holy Spirit will accomplish in you, " to-day, if you will hear his voice."

"God now commandeth all men every where to repent."
This command is laid as a terror across your path; you
cannot proceed one step farther in an irreligious course
without trampling it under foot; without practically saying, 'God commands me to repent, but I will not repent:
the Holy Ghost saith, hear his voice to-day, but to-day I
will not hear it.' If to-morrow's rising sun find you out
of the narrow way of life, it will find you where God for-
bids you to be on pain of his severest displeasure.—Remember eternity is at hand.—Time speeds away.

> "No winds along the hills can flee
> So swiftly or so smooth as he;
> Like fiery steed—from stage to stage,
> He bears us on from youth to age,
> Then plunges in the fearful sea
> Of fathomless eternity."

Let the faithful in Christ Jesus, into whose hands this
narrative may come, be stirred up to earnest, persevering
prayer, that the Lord's work may be successfully carried
on in Scotland, even the great work of quickening the
dead, justifying the guilty, and sanctifying the ungodly.
Let Christians throughout the land unite for this purpose.
Let congregations unite to implore the divine blessing on
the labours of their pastors. It is in this manner that the
arm of the Lord must be awakened; and when societies
for prayer are multiplied, we may be assured that a day of
power is at hand. The showers which have before refreshed our land will refresh it yet again, and the gospel
will anew be preached with the Spirit sent down from
above, making ministers divinely wise to win souls to
Christ, and sending them forth in all corners and churches
of this land, with as full a blessing of the gospel of Christ
as Scotland or America has ever before experienced.

Compiled from ROBE's Narrative of Revival at Kilsyth—GILLIES'
Historical Collection and Life of Whitefield.

REVIVALS OF RELIGION.

No. II.

KILSYTH, 1742-3.

WHEN the Saviour had nearly "finished the work" the Father had given him to do, and when about to be invested as Mediator with the glory which he had with the Father before the world was, he comforted his disconsolate followers by telling them, that when he went away, he would send the Comforter, who would lead them into all Truth, and who would abide with them for ever. And, after his resurrection, before he bade them a final adieu, he left with them, and through them to all his followers in every age, this animating promise—"Lo, I am with you alway, even unto the end of the world." Every christian is aware how remarkably these promises were accomplished, in the experience of the primitive church. "Jesus Christ is the same, yesterday, to day, and for ever." Since the memorable day of Pentecost he has repeatedly, and sometimes not less remarkably, fulfilled his gracious promise of "the gift of the Holy Ghost." Perhaps no country in the world since the days of the Apostles, has been so signally blessed, in this respect, as Scotland. Many are the instances in which Divine influence has descended "as dew upon the tender herb, and as the showers upon the grass, "on this hitherto privileged and happy land. If the Jews of old, when they reached "the other side Jordan," were required frequently to recount "the acts of the Lord," and the way by which their fathers had been led, surely it is most befitting that the spiritual seed of Jacob should recollect and commemorate the manifestations of Divine grace, in past ages, towards the true Israel of God. The remembering of God's dealings with his ancient people was intended to benefit the descendants of those who had been the subjects of them; so, perhaps, the present attempt to record "God's mighty acts," towards His spiritual Israel in this land, may, by the blessing of the Spirit, stir up some of the present generation in faith and in fervency to desire even "greater things than these."

It was early in the year 1742, when the Spirit of God remarkably visited the parish of Cambuslang, then under the pastoral care of the Rev. Mr. M'Culloch. It was computed that, by his instrumentality, aided by many pious ministers, about four hundred individuals were brought to the knowledge of the truth as it is in Jesus. This remarkable display of the Mediator's power awakened great joy in the hearts of God's people, and stirred up many pious ministers and people in other parishes to earnest persevering prayer that the Lord would carry on His work, and refresh his weary heritage over the land. Among the many godly ministers who frequently visited Cambuslang on this memorable occasion was the Rev. Mr. Robe, minister of the neighbouring parish of Kilsyth. Like Mr. M'Culloch, he was a man of prayer, deeply aware of the responsibility attending his office, and anxiously solicitous for the eternal welfare of his people. Every time he visited Cambuslang he seems to have returned to his own charge as if "anointed with fresh oil," resolutely determined to know nothing among them but "Jesus Christ, and him crucified." By this time he had laboured in the parish of Kilsyth for the space of thirty years, without being aware of any remarkable success having accompanied his ministrations. During that period, the parish had been visited with a severe fever, by which many, particularly of the godly, were suddenly cut off. That visitation was followed by a famine, and shortly after, in the summer of 1733, great loss was sustained by a destructive storm of thunder and lightning; but, instead of these judgments leading the people to think of God, whose displeasure they had incurred, and to seek Him "with weeping and with supplication," wickedness seemed to increase. Mr. Robe, in his narrative, testifies that no one appeared to be affected with sin, the cause of all the evils that were complained of. On the contrary, the Societies for prayer declined, the love of many waxed cold, the spirit of formality seemed to prevail, and open transgression greatly abounded. In these painful circumstances the good man betook himself to prayer in behalf of his people, and continued still most faithfully to set before them "life and death—the blessing and the curse." In the year 1740, he commenced a series of practical discourses on the doctrine of regeneration. He explained and applied, with all faithfulness and scriptural simplicity, the nature, the importance, the necessity, the evidences of this spiritual transformation, and although these discourses were listened to with apparent seriousness, yet no visible effects followed at the time. When Cambuslang and other parishes were sharing so copiously of the Divine influence, it was matter of grief and discouragement to Mr. Robe that not one of his people seemed as yet at all to be awakened. He continued to wrestle much in prayer, and still with affectionate earnestness to exhibit to his people a full and free salvation. " The effectual fervent prayer of a righteous man availeth much." Like Jacob, he wrestled, and, like Israel, he prevailed—The Lord did in due time send a " plenteous rain." The first symptoms were the reviving of many of the meetings for prayer, the institution of some new similar associations, and particularly of one composed exclusively of females, from ten to sixteen years of age. These movements were hailed as the harbingers of brighter days.

Mr. Willison of Dundee, " whose praise is in the gospel throughout all the churches," being on a visit to Cambuslang, spent a few days at Kilsyth, on his way home. Being requested to preach, he did so, and delivered " a distinct, plain, and moving sermon," from these words:—"He brought me up also out of a horrible pit, out of the miry clay, and set my feet upon a rock, and established my goings." Many of those who were afterwards effectually awakened dated their first serious concern about their souls, from hearing that sermon. On the Sabbath following, 18th April, 1742, Mr. Robe preached from these words :—" My little children, of whom I travail in birth again until Christ be formed in you." He experienced more than usual tenderness in reading the text, and could not refrain from tears. On the Sabbath immediately following, one woman was awakened to a very distressing sight of her sinfulness and consequent exposure to misery. She was observed by some in the congregation to be under great uneasiness. When the congregation dismissed, she was not able to proceed on her way home, and soon after was found in a field, crying out like the jailer, " what shall I do to be saved?" She was brought back to the minister, who conversed with her for a considerable time. She said that in hearing the sermon she was made to see that she was unlike Jesus Christ, and like the Devil, and altogether in a state of unregeneracy. She had strong impressions

of the greatness of the wrath of God, to which, on account
of sin, she felt herself liable. She parted with Mr. Robe
considerably composed. She continued for some time to
endure occasionally, very great mental anguish, but soon
after obtained sensible relief, by an " apprehension of the
mercy of God in Christ." On Sabbath, the 9th of May
following, five persons were awakened to a distressing
sight of their sinful and lost estate. Mr. Robe, and the
praying people around, fondly cherished the hope that
this might be but as a few drops before the plentiful rain.

And now the period of peculiar favour to this parish
was come—the time that God had set. Mr. Robe in his
narrative states,—" On May 16, I preached, as I have
done for some time, on Gal. iv. 19 : ' My little children,
of whom I travail in birth until Christ be formed in you.'
While pressing all the unregenerate to seek to have Christ
formed in them, an extraordinary power of the Divine
Spirit accompanied the word preached. There was a great
mourning in the congregation, as for an only son. Many
cried out, and these not only women, but some strong and
stout-hearted young men. After the congregation was
dismissed," continues Mr. Robe, " an attempt was made
to get the distressed into my barn, but their number being
so great this was impossible, and I was obliged to convene
them in the kirk. I sung a psalm and prayed with them,
but when I essayed to speak to them I could not be heard,
so great were their bitter cries, groans, and the voice of
their weeping. After this, I requested that they might
come into my closet, one by one. I sent for the Rev. Mr.
John Oughterson, minister of Cumbernauld, who immediately came to assist me in dealing with the distressed.
In the meantime, I appointed psalms to be sung with those
in the kirk, and that the precentor and two or three of the
elders should pray with them. The noise of the distressed
was heard from afar. It was pleasant to hear those who
had been in a state of enmity with God, despisers of Jesus
Christ, and Satan's contented slaves, crying out for mercy;
—some, that they were lost and undone;—others, ' what
shall we do to be saved;' others, praising God for this day,
and for awakening them; and not a few, not only weeping
and crying for themselves, but for their graceless relations.
And yet it would have moved the hardest heart, that many
of them, like the Israelites under Pharaoh's oppression,
hearkened not when I spoke unto them, they were so over-

whelmed with anguish of spirit, because of the spiritual bondage they felt they were under—There appeared about thirty awakened this day, belonging to this and the neighbouring congregations. About twenty of them belonged to this parish. Some few to the parish of Campsie, and the remainder to that of Kirkintilloch. But I have found since, in conversing with the distressed, that the number of the awakened far exceeds thirty."

"On the Wednesday immediately following this day ot the Redeemer's power, there was a sermon for the first time on a week day. Mr. Warden, minister of Campsie, and Mr. M'Laurin, one of the ministers of Glasgow, preached on the occasion. The number of the awakened this day was as great as on the Lord's day. The greater number was from the parish of Kirkintilloch; there were also some from the parishes of Campsie and Cumbernauld. Nor did this movement of Divine grace soon terminate. The blessed work of conviction and conversion went on. The Redeemer did " ride prosperously because of truth, and meekness, and righteousness,"—His " arrows were sharp in the heart of the King's enemies. The number of the awakened, belonging to this parish, amounted this week to forty."

When the Revival commenced, such was the desire of the people to hear the word of God, that, as has been just stated, it was found necessary to institute a week-day lecture. Wednesday was the day selected for that purpose; and on that day there were sometimes two and even three discourses. Monday, Tuesday, Thursday, and Friday, were appropriated for conversing with the spiritually distressed. Notwithstanding such abundant labours, Mr. Robe was enabled to persevere—his bodily health suffered not, and his inward man prospered day by day. His friends sometimes tried to persuade him to relax his excessive labours, but, growing love to Jesus, intense compassion for perishing souls, ardent zeal for the promotion of God's glory, constrained him to persevere in his arduous but interesting duties. " It soon became," says he, " the pleasantest work in which I ever engaged. Though I was wearied when I went to bed, yet, like the labouring man, my rest was sweet to me. The Lord gave me the sleep of his beloved, and I was fresh by the morning. The way of the Lord hath been my life and my strength."

The ordinance of the Supper was as usual, dispensed

on the second Sabbath of June, and was attended by the
happiest results in the experience of many. The blessed
work of conviction and conversion continued greatly to
increase after that solemn communion service, and it was
intimated to the minister in the middle of September following, that a general desire existed among the people for
another and an early opportunity of observing that ordinance. After much prayer and conference on the part
both of the minister and the people, it was resolved that
the death of our Lord should be a second time celebrated
that year; which was accordingly done on the third Sabbath of October. the account given by Mr. Robe of that
interesting solemnity is truly heart stirring. "I was assisted
on the occasion by the Rev. Mr. M'Laurin of Glasgow,
Mr. James Warden of Calder, Mr. John Warden of Campsie,
Mr. James Burnside of Kirkintilloch, Mr. James Mackie
of St. Ninians, Mr. John Smith of Larbert, Mr. Spiers of
Linlithgow, Mr. Thomas Gillespie of Carnock, Mr. Hunter
of Saline, Mr. M'Culloch of Cambuslang, and Mr. Porteous
of Monivaird. Upon the Fast-day, sermon was in the fields
to a very numerous and attentive audience, by three ministers, without any intermission, because of the shortness of
the day. Upon the Friday evening there was sermon in
the kirk, and there was a good deal of concern among the
people. Upon Saturday there was sermon both in the
kirk and in the fields. Upon the Lord's day the public
service began about half-past eight in the morning, and
continued without intermission till half-past eight in the
evening. I preached the action sermon, by the Divine
direction and assistance, from Eph. ii. 7. ' That in the
ages to come he might show the exceeding riches of his
grace, in his kindness towards us, through Christ Jesus.'
There were about twenty-two services, each consisting of
about seventy persons. The evening sermon began immediately after the last table-service. And though I desired
that the congregation in the fields should be dismissed after
the last service, yet they chose rather to continue together
till all was over. During all the services there was the
most desirable frame and observable concern among the
people, that had ever been any where seen. It began to
be considerable, when Mr. Warden of Campsie preached,
and it continued and greatly increased while Mr. Spiers
preached, who concluded the public work of the day in
the fields. On Monday there were sermons both in the

kirk and in the fields. There was a good deal of observable
concern; and several were brought under spiritual distress in the fields. In the evening, two ministers preached
to the numerous distressed convened in the kirk. On
Tuesday morning there was a sermon preached, and a discourse by another minister, containing suitable instructions
and directions both to the awakened, and to those who
had never attained to any sight or sense of their sin and
danger. The spiritual fruits of this solemn and extraordinary dispensation of Word and Sacrament were truly animating. Many secure sinners were awakened. Zion's
mighty King brought the wheel of the law over them, and
sent them home with broken and contrite hearts. Some
who came hither in a state of spiritual distress and law-work,
felt such a time of the Mediator's power as enabled them
to embrace Jesus Christ with such distinctness, as to know
that they had done it. Many had the love of Christ so
shed abroad in their hearts by the Holy Ghost, that they
could not contain, but were constrained to break forth in
floods of tears in the most significant expressions of their
own vileness and unworthiness, and of the deep sense they
had of the exceeding riches of God's grace, in his kindness
towards them by Christ Jesus."

It is delightful to contemplate the solid nature of this
work of Revival. It was far removed from enthusiastic
fanaticism on the one hand, and presumptuous Antinomi-
anism on the other. Although some who seemed to be
awakened ultimately fell away, yet the experience of many
made it unequivocally manifest, that "the Lord himself
had given the word." Deep humility, hatred of all sin,
love of holiness, aspirations after conformity to the image
of God, fervent prayers and endeavours that others might
be brought to the same views and the same enjoyments,
characterised the greater number of the individuals with
whom Mr. Robe was called to converse. Indeed, the views
of sin, and of the way of salvation, entertained by the individuals brought under the power of this blessed work of
the Spirit, were, generally speaking, of the most scriptural
and enlightened description. One man being asked " what
he took closing with Christ to be;" made this most intelligent reply:—"I take closing with Christ to be a receiving
of Him as a Prophet, to teach me the way of salvation;
as a Priest to atone for me, and to be my righteousness in
the sight of God; and, as a King, to rule over me, and to

subdue sin and corruption in me : and that without Christ's righteousness imputed, I can never be accepted in the sight of God." One woman, after she was brought distinctly to receive, and rest alone upon Christ for salvation, thus expressed herself:—"Worldly thoughts are away from me now, and oh that they would never return again! Ten thousand worlds could not give me the love and joy with which Christ now fills me." When asked some questions by Mr. Robe, she said, "Sir, though you put questions to me, as was done to Peter, Christ, who knows my heart, knows that I do love Him, and I am resolved, in the strength of imparted promised grace, to show my love to Him by keeping His commandments." She sometimes gave utterance to such words as these—"He is my sure portion, whom I have chosen for ever. Oh, what hath he done for me! I desire to have all the world brought to Him, that they too may partake of His rich and sovereign grace."

Although the greater number, like the awakened at the day of Pentecost, or like the convicted jailer at Philippi, were made to cry out, under a sense of sin and apprehension of coming wrath, and could not conceal their distress, yet many were brought to Jesus in a more gentle and silent manner, whose cases were not made known to Mr. Robe till they had obtained peace in believing. Two or three instances of this kind may be given, nearly in Mr. Robe's own words, from among the many that might be quoted:—A woman who was brought to concern on 16th May, waited upon Mr. Robe the following week, manifesting great anxiety for the salvation of her soul. "I was," says he, "much pleased with the character of her convictions, with her knowledge, and the longing desires she expressed after Jesus Christ. I said to her, 'essay to accept of Christ, bestir yourself, rise up at his call, and invite Him to enter into your heart, into your soul.' Without intending or meaning what she did, she arose with great composure, stood and prayed in a most scriptural style. She acknowledged sin, original and actual, her utter want of righteousness, the wonderfulness of God's patience to her. She prayed for mercy to be drawn to Jesus Christ, and that she might be clothed with His white raiment. Sometimes in her address, she would say—'Sweet Jesus;' 'He is precious;' 'He is altogether lovely.' She first came to sensible relief from a sermon I preached on John xvi. 10, 'Of righteousness, because I go to my Father, and ye see me no more.' In her return home that day, these words were strongly impressed on her mind—'My heart is fixed, O God, my heart is fixed; I will sing and give praise.' She fell down upon her knees; her heart being filled with joy in the Lord, and her mouth with His praise."—

—" C. D. came first under convictions by hearing the doctrine of regeneration stated, as it is the writing of God's law upon the sinner's heart, from Heb. viii. 10. He was made distinctly to see that it was not as yet written upon his heart, and that if he would be happy hereafter, it was indispensably necessary that it should be so. Upon the evening of the day when he received his first impressions, he conversed with a friend concerning the resurrection, the general judgment, and the sad state in which impenitent sinners must be throughout eternity. By such converse his impressions were deepened. Every sermon and every awakening experienced by his neighbours was blessed for the same end. He told me that he could apply to himself the greater part of a sermon he heard from me concerning the Spirit's convincing the world of sin; such as, that he usually begins with one sin, and after that proceeds to convince of particular sins. He was convinced of the sins of his heart, and of the evil nature of sin. He was not so much distressed about sin, as exposing him to hell, but he felt particularly grieved as it was an insult offered to a holy God. He got such a sight of the filthiness of sin, as to loathe himself on account of it. He was also convinced of the great sin of unbelief, of the sinfulness of the least thought of iniquity, though not consented thereto; of the evil of self-conceit, a sense of the sinfulness of which stuck as long with him, as he termed it, as any thing else. He was also sensible of his inability to help himself, of his own want of righteousness, and that he could not work out a righteousness for himself. He was brought to see the sufficiency of Christ's righteousness, and that He, to use his own words, was always ready, if he would but trust in Him. Seeing that he had not informed any one of his spiritual distress till he got relief by believing in Christ, I asked what it was that kept up his spirit under fear and trouble of mind, continuing so long. He told me that when his heart was like to burst in prayer, that word came constantly in his mind, and encouraged him to wait for the Lord with patience and hope:— I waited patiently for the Lord, and He inclined unto me, and heard my cry.' His first relief came in this manner. In the Society for Prayer of which he had become a member, he inquired, 'What was the most proper exercise for a person under convictions?' to which it was replied by a very judicious Christian, ' That it was to behold the Lamb of God.' which he essayed to do.—When I gave, in a public discourse, the marks of those who had Christ formed in them, he said that by the help of the Spirit he could apply them all to himself, and that during prayer and after sermon he was in a frame surprising to himself; that his whole heart and affections went out in closing with Jesus Christ, and that he was filled with rejoicing and wonder at His love."

" R. S. was first touched with convictions on the Lord's day, May 16. He heard sermons upon the Wednesday at Kilsyth, and upon Thursday at Kirkintilloch. He spent the greater part of the last mentioned evening in the fields, crying out under a deep sense of sin. He came to me on the following day in great mental distress. He had a distressing sight of particular sins, such as Sabbath-breaking, cursing, swearing, evil thoughts, &c. He was grieved for sin as an offence against God ; and said with great earnestness, he would give a thousand worlds for Christ. He saw that he had a vile corrupt nature, and mourned over the sin of so long despising Christ through unbelief. I endeavoured to instruct him in the nature of faith and the way of salvation through Jesus Christ. On a subsequent occasion, when conversing with him, he said he had endeavoured to close with a whole Christ in all his offices, and counts all things but loss and dung, for the excellency of the knowledge of Jesus Christ, and that he may win him. He said that he had now an inclination to Christ, and that his heart flutters in him like a bird when he thinks of him."

It is emphatically said by an inspired writer, that " the grace of God which bringeth salvation, teaches to deny ungodliness and worldly lusts, and to live soberly, righteously, and godly, in this present evil world." This declaration of holy Scripture, received remarkable illustration at Kilsyth. The number of individuals who were awakened in the parish, and who afterwards publicly professed the faith of Christ, was upwards of three hundred ; and by various authentic documents, recorded in Mr. Robe's Narrative, it is ascertained that the life and conversation of these, with fewer exceptions than might have been expected, were such as became the gospel. The moral influence on the parish generally, was remarkable.

Mr. Robe thus writes—" Among the instances of the good fruits of this work upon the people, may be mentioned visible reformation from many open sins, particularly cursing, swearing, and drinking. In social meetings, edifying conversation has taken place of what was frothy, foolish, or censorious. Instead of worldly and common discourse on the Lord's day, there is that which is spiritual and good to the use of edifying. There is little of what was formerly common, strolling about the fields, or sitting idle at the doors of their house on that holy day. There is a general desire after public ordinances. Before this, I could never prevail with the best to attend the preaching of the Word during the week, and therefore could have no stated weekly meeting for expounding; now, however, they desire it, and the generality of the people attend as regularly as upon the Lord's day. The worship of God is set up and maintained in many families who formerly neglected it. There are many new societies for prayer, composed of individuals of all ages, and not only of those who have been lately awakened, but of those who before had a character for seriousness. Former feuds and animosities are in a great measure laid aside and forgot, and this hath been the most peaceable summer amongst neighbours that was ever known in this parish. I have heard little or nothing of that pilfering and stealing that was so frequent before this work began. Yea, there have been several instances of restitution, and some of these showing consciences of more than ordinary tenderness. The change on the face of our public meetings for worship is visible: there was never such attention and seriousness seen in them as now. The change is observed by every one who formerly knew the parish. One observing person said to me, that if there was no more gained by this wonderful work of the Spirit, there was at least a great increase of morality."

Such is a short sketch of the remarkable outpouring of the Spirit of God at Kilsyth during the year 1742–3. It furnishes one among the many emblems of that more " plentiful rain" with which the millennial glory shall be ushered in. When the past history of the world and of the church is contemplated, it is refreshing to find such verdant spots amidst the spiritual sterility that every where abounds. And when viewing the present aspect of society, so luke-warm and so secure, it is delightful to anticipate with certainty the predicted period, when, in the metaphoric language of Scripture, " the wilderness and the solitary place shall be glad, and the desert shall rejoice and blossom as the rose." The outpouring of the Holy Spirit, by which alone this change can be effected, is matter of promise, and matter of prophecy. The prayer of faith works wonders. The plea of the finished work of Emmanuel is irresistible. Encouraged then by the promises, the predictions, and the arguments of Scripture, let every true wrestler at the throne of grace adopt the resolution of the Prophet—" For Zion's sake will I not hold my peace, and for Jerusalem's sake I will not rest, until the righteousness thereof go forth as brightness, and the salvation thereof as a lamp that burneth."

While secret prayer for the descent of the Holy Spirit is thus earnestly pressed, small concerts for prayer are at the same time no less urgently recommended. Such meetings preceded, accompanied, and followed the Revival of 1742. Jesus still reigns " a Prince and a Saviour"—" a Priest upon his throne"—ready to subdue the rebellious heart of man by the efficacy of his own sacrifice. The love of Jehovah is still overflowing. The resources of the Spirit are still equal to the conversion of a world: one breathing from HIM would make our people live. O then let God's people unite together—let them speak often one to another: He will hearken and hear! Let them give Him no rest till he establish, and till he make Jerusalem a praise in the earth!

REVIVALS OF RELIGION.

No. III.

Baldernoch, Kirkintilloch, Muthill, &c. 1742-3.

An attempt has been made, in the two preceding numbers of this series, to give a sketch of the state of religion in Cambuslang and Kilsyth, during the years 1742–3; and in the present it is proposed to give a brief account of the progress of the truth in other parts of Scotland during the same period; for the work of religion, revived in these parishes, could not but excite great interest in the districts and congregations around them. Multitudes flocked from all quarters; some attracted by curiosity, others to gain spiritual refreshment, and not a few to mock and to ridicule. At the memorable dispensation of the Lord's supper at Cambuslang, for instance, on the third Sabbath of August, 1742, there were present many individuals from Irvine, Kilmarnock, Dreghorn, and other parishes in that neighbourhood; and it was afterwards ascertained that about sixty of these returned home seriously impressed with a sense of their sinfulness and misery, and not a few rejoicing in the grace of the gospel. These individuals were instrumental in awakening others. Prayer meetings were established; and then, by the preaching of the gospel, many other converts were added to those who had been awakened at Cambuslang.

In the parishes eastward of Kilsyth the revival was little felt. The people were keenly engaged in discussing the externals of Christianity, and were thereby prevented from studying very minutely the doctrines of vital religion. It has been found that keen party spirit almost necessarily destroys spirituality of mind. An anxious desire to obtain connection with a sect, is too frequently substituted for earnest solicitude to gain union with Jesus, the Saviour. Nevertheless, there were a few witnesses for God raised up even in these parishes. In Denny and Larbert, particularly, this was the case. The Almighty Spirit triumphed over the carnality of many nominal professors, and rendered them the living members of Christ. Not a few gainsayers were reclaimed, whose lives afterwards furnished a practical and ocular demonstration, that the work was of God, and not of man.

In the parish of Torphichen, to the eastward of Linlithgow, at that time under the ministry of Mr. Bonar, seven persons were awakened at the dispensation of the Supper of the Lord, on the first Sabbath of August, 1742, who afterwards were enabled to give scriptural evidence of being in Christ by a living faith.

The case of the parish of Baldernock deserves to be particularly noticed. Few of the people had visited those places in which the revivals had originated; and although for some years there had been no regular pastor, yet about ninety individuals were brought under the quickening influence of the Spirit of promise. Mr. Wallace, who had previously laboured amongst them in holy things for about fifty years, had been faithful and zealous; and perhaps the many conversions that now took place, might be remotely traced to his ministrations. The seed which lies long concealed may spring up in an abundant harvest. But in the absence of a regular ministry, God, who can accomplish His purposes of mercy with weak as well as with powerful means, raised up and qualified Mr. James Forsyth, who occupied the humble but honourable station of parochial schoolmaster, as the instrument of carrying forward in that parish, the good work that had made such advances in the surrounding country. He was evidently a good man. He had been long distinguished for godliness. His experience of the preciousness of Christ, could not but prompt him to embrace the opportunity, which his profession furnished, of diffusing the knowledge of that Name, and of that Salvation, which he knew to be essential to the true happiness of the people with whom he was brought in contact. He partook of the joy with which the news of God's dealings with his church was received by such as had themselves tasted that the Lord is gracious; and in the peculiar circumstances of the parish, he endeavoured, by every means in his power, to infuse the same spiritual life among the people. He spoke, more especially to the young, with earnestness and affection about their lost condition by nature and practice, about the love of God manifested in the gift of his Son for the salvation of sinners ready to perish; and the Holy Spirit was pleased to convey these simple but impressive truths to the hearts of his interesting charge, who, in their turn, were enabled to leave a testimony to the truth, in the consciences of the adult population. Would there were many such teachers of youth! Would that they felt that they and their youthful charge shall stand together in the judgment, and must render an account of their important stewardship! Religious instruction was made to hold a prominent place in the school under the charge of Mr. Forsyth; and for the encouragement of all in like circumstances, these instructions were rendered instrumental for the conversion of many. God countenanced his feeble endeavours, and made him the honoured instrument of winning many souls to Christ. His own account of the matter is detailed in letters to Mr. Robe, and will be felt deeply interesting and animating by all who have any love for ardent piety or disinterested zeal. In a letter dated 17th July, 1742, he thus writes—" Since the first of February last, I endeavoured, to the utmost of my power, to instruct the children under my charge in the first principles of religion—that they were born in a state of sin and misery, and strangers to God by nature. I pressed them, with every argument I could thing of, to give up their sinful ways, and flee to Jesus Christ by faith and repentance; and by the blessing of God, my efforts were not made in vain. Glory to His holy-name, that that which was spoken in much weakness, was accompanied by the power of His Holy Spirit. I likewise warned them against the commission of known sin. I told them the danger of persisting contrary to the voice of conscience, and the plain dictates of the word of God; assuring them, that if they did so, their sin would one day find them out. These exhortations, frequently repeated, made at last some impression on their young hearts. This was used as a means in God's hand for bringing the elder sort to a more serious concern, and a greater diligence in religious duties. Qne of the school boys, who went to Cambuslang in March, was the first awakened. He, in a short time thereafter, asked permission to meet with two or three of the other boys in the school-room, for the purpose of praying and singing psalms. I had great pleasure in granting this request. Very soon after, a few more of the boys manifested deep concern for their souls; and in fourteen days after the opening of this youthful prayer meeting, ten or twelve were hopefully awakened; none of them were above thirteen years of age —a few of them were so young as eight or nine. These associated together for devotional duties. Their love for these services increased; so much so, that they sometimes met three times a-day,—early in the morning,—at noon, during the interval of school hours,—and in the evening. These soon forsook all their childish fancies and plays, and were known to their school companions by their general appearance, by their walk and conversation. All this had a happy effect upon the other children. Many were awakened through their means. They became remarkable for tenderness of conscience. A word of terror occurring in their lessons would sometimes make them cry out and weep bitterly. Some of them could give a most intelligent account of their experience of divine truth. They were sensible of the sin of their nature, of their actual transgressions, and even of the sin of unbelief; for when I would exhort them to believe in Christ, who was both able and willing to save them to the uttermost, they would reply, in the most affecting terms, that they knew He was both able and willing, but their hearts were so hard that they could not believe aright of themselves, till God gave them the new heart—that they could do nothing for their hard hearts."

It has been often illustrated, that "out of the mouths of babes and sucklings God perfects praise." What heart that reads this narrative can feel unmoved at the striking illustration thus furnished of this scripture saying, in the case of the youth of the parish of Baldernoch, under the care of Mr. Forsyth! Who would not pray that all teachers of youth were blessed with piety like his, with zeal like his, with success like his!

Respecting the people in general, Mr. F. thus writes— "Some were awakened at Cambuslang, others at Calder and Kirkintilloch, but the greater number at the private meetings for prayer held in the parish. These meetings were held twice a-week, and all were admitted who chose to attend."—These meetings were eminently countenanced. Many who attended were blessed with the communications of Divine grace, and made to experience the image and the earnest of the fellowship that is above. "Two young women," says Mr. Forsyth, "who had been at Cambuslang, and who brought back an evil report, saying, that they wondered what made the people cry out, on the 22d of June, came to one of these meetings in Baldernoch, as was supposed, with no good design. Before a quarter of an hour had elapsed, they were brought under serious convictions, and continued in distress during the remaining exercises of the evening."

These details of the awakening in Baldernoch furnish an impressive commentary on these words of scripture— "Not by might, nor by power, but by my Spirit, saith the Lord:" "I will have mercy on whom I will have mercy and I will have compassion on whom I will have compassion"—and should stimulate every Christian, in his own sphere, to labour for Christ, trusting that the Divine Spirit will come "and leave a blessing behind Him."

Respecting the case of Baldernoch, Mr. Robe has the following judicious remarks;—" I have been the more particular, that we who are ministers of the gospel may learn not to be lifted up by any success we may have in our ministrations; though the Lord maketh especially the preaching of the word an effectual means of convincing and converting sinners, and of building up them who are converted, yet he also blesseth the reading of the word, Christian communion, and religious education, by parents, schoolmasters, and others, for the same blessed ends, and, also that he sometimes makes use of weak and inconsiderable instruments for beginning and carrying on a good work upon the souls of men, while men of great gifts are not so successful. The people are not the less careful to attend upon public ordinances ; their meetings do not interfere with the public means of grace in their own congregation, nor with the same privileges in the neighbouring congregations, when deprived of them in their own church, in consequence of there being at present no regular minister."

At the parish of Killearn, about sixteen miles north from Glasgow, at that time under the pastoral inspection of Mr. James Bain, there was a considerable awakening at the dispensation of the Lord's supper, on the third Sabbath of July, 1742. This was particularly the case on the Monday, when sermons were delivered by Mr. Michael Potter, professor of divinity in the University of Glasgow, and Mr. Mackie, minister of St. Ninians.

There were about a hundred awakened in the parish of Campsie; and about the same number in the parish of Calder, in the immediate neighbourhood. The circumstances connected with the revival at Calder are somewhat remarkable. Mr. Warden, the minister, was accustomed to give a weekly lecture in a small village at some distance from the church. The attendance had become so very inconsiderable, that he had resolved to discontinue it. The evening he went to make this announcement, to his great amazement he found the room crowded. Dismayed at such a multitude, and as he had prepared no subject of exposition, he retired into a wood at a little distance, earnestly imploring Divine direction and blessing. Immediately he returned to the people, and preached from these words which had been suggested to his mind while in the wood—" Unto you, O men, I call; and my voice is to the sons of men," Prov. viii. 4. From this text he opened up the fulness, the freeness, the grace of the gospel proclamation. The Holy Spirit accompanied the word spoken with power. Many were brought under His humbling influence, and ultimately made to bow to the sceptre of Jesus. On a subsequent occasion there were about fourteen persons brought under great concern and anxiety about their spiritual and eternal state.

About this time about sixteen young people in the town of Kirkintilloch were observed to meet in a barn for prayer. This took place at the suggestion of one of the older boys, and was cordially acceded to by the rest. This incident coming to be known, seemed to make deep impressions both upon old and young. The minister of the parish was rejoiced by this movement, inquired after the little prayer meeting, and frequently joined the society, for giving direction and instruction. At the dispensation of the Lord's supper, in May following, Mr. Maclaurin of Glasgow, and Mr. Robe of Kilsyth, preached on the fast-day preparatory to the celebration of that solemnity. Mr. Burnside, the minister of the parish, preached in the evening of the same day. The work of conviction was general and powerful. In the words of Mr. Robe, "Zion's mighty King did appear in His glory and majesty, and His arrows were sharp in the heart of His enemies." About a hundred and twenty applied to the minister, anxiously seeking the way to Zion, evidently with their faces thitherward. About the same time there were fourteen or fifteen awakened at Cumbernauld, under the preaching of Mr. Whitefield; and about eighty individuals by the ordinary ministrations of their own pastor Mr. Oughterson.

At the dispensation of the supper, in St. Ninians, on the first Sabbath of August of the same year, there were several awakened by means of the sermons on the Saturday many more on Sabbath, and a far greater number on the Monday, which was, on the testimony of Mr. Robe, "one of the greatest days of the Mediator's power ever beheld." On Thursday immediately following, at the usual week-day lecture, a considerable number more were awakened. Mr. Mackie, the minister of the parish, was instrumental in leading many of the inquirers to the Lamb of God, who taketh away the sin of the world. Some time after, Mr. Mackie states, "that impressions upon the people are far 'rom wearing off. Their behaviour is such that their ene-mies themselves cannot find fault with. It gives me great pleasure to hear them pray and converse. Our audience is most attentive to the preaching of the word."

In the parish of Gargunnoch there were about a hun-dred awakened, the greater number of whom were brought to a state of concern for their souls, while attending the dis-pensation of the supper at Kilsyth, on the second Sabbath of July, or the dispensation of that ordinance at Campsie, on the last Sabbath of that month, or at St. Ninians, on the first Sabbath of August. At the week-day lecture, on the 5th of August, there were eighteen awakened; and in the week following many more. In a letter of date 17th March, the following year, Mr. Warden, the minister of the parish, writes—" The concern in a great measure con-tinues; fellowship meetings increase; and even the meetings for prayer among the children. The impression among the people, in general, is still apparent, by a diligent at-tendance upon ordinances, love to our God and Redeemer, and to all the children of our Lord's family; crying to Christ, and rejoicing in Him; and all this associated with a sober and blameless walk and conversation. A few are under spiritual concern in the parish of Kippen, and there is some stir in the parish of Monivaird."

About the same time, this wondrous work of the Lord extended to the parish of Muthill, in Perthshire. Mr. Halley, the minister, gives the following account, in a let-ter, addressed to Mr. Robe, dated March, 1743. " The work of God is going forward in this parish. Many seem truly awakened to a sense of their condition, as connected with eternity. All those with whom I have conversed, appeared to be touched to the very quick, the arrows of the Almighty shot to their very hearts; trembling like the Jailer, crying out against sin, and breathing and thirsting after a Saviour. My bowels were moved for them, and,

I hope, the bowels of a compassionate Redeemer were yearning over them, when they were with Ephraim be-moaning themselves. As a token for future good, a pray-ing disposition among the people, not only continues, but is upon the increase. Thirteen Societies for prayer, have been recently instituted, and a new one is about to be established. I cannot express how much I am charmed with the young people. They have now three prayer Societies. The members of one of these made me a most agreeable visit upon the first Monday of the year, a day which young people especially, usually spend in mirth and folly. Upwards of forty attended, and continued in prayer and other exercises, till about ten at night. And oh! to hear the young lambs crying after the great Shepherd, to hear them pouring out their souls with such fervour, with such beautiful expressions, with such copiousness and ful-ness, did not only strike me with admiration, but melted me into tears. I wished in my heart that all contradictors, gainsayers, and blasphemers of this work of God, had been where I was that night." In a subsequent letter, Mr. Halley thus writes—" The concern in hearing the word still continues, though not with such a noise and outcry-ing as formerly. And though the public awakenings are not so discernible as they were sometime since, yet few Sabbaths pass, but there are some pricked in their hearts, and with great anguish of spirit, crying, What shall we do? A law-work is still severe and of long continuance with many, but the Lord is supporting, helping to wait, and keeping them thirsting after relief in Christ."

In the parish of Crief, then under the pastoral care of the Rev. Mr. Drummond, there were many awakened, and ultimately made happy, in knowing and believing the truth. Several praying Societies were formed.

In all the parishes in which this Revival made any pro-gress, a corresponding increase of practical godliness imme-diately became apparent. Fellowship Meetings were insti-tuted, family religion every where revived, Sabbath desecra-tion was discountenanced, open profanity, for the most part, disappeared. The virtues of honesty, industry, and so-briety, characterised the people, and amongst the peculiar subjects of the revivals, instances of restitution not unfre-quently occurred. These fruits of holiness must have tend-ed to remove the cavils of the " enemy and the avenger," during that interesting period, and to this day, attested as

they are by irrefragable evidence, furnish the most satisfying proof, that the work was of God, and not of man.
" Godly sorrow for sin, universal hatred at it, renouncing
their own righteousness, and embracing the righteousness
of God, by faith in Jesus Christ, embracing him in all his
offices, universal reformation of life, a superlative love to
the blessed Redeemer, love to all who bear his image, love
towards all men, even to enemies, earnest desires and
prayers for the conversion of all others :"—" These," says
Mr. Robe, " are the happy fruits of this blessed work, and
sufficiently demonstrate that it is of the operation of the
Spirit of God."

This may be better illustrated by one or two examples
of individual experience, taken from Mr. Robe's narrative. " L. M., aged about twenty-eight years, and formerly of a blameless life, was awakened by conversing
with his brother under spiritual distress. On that night
he was so deeply affected that he could not sleep. Next
morning, his distress was increased by reading that passage of ' Alleine's Alarm,' in which he discourseth of
God's being an enemy to unconverted sinners, which
passage he met with at the first opening of the book."
Mr. Robe continues—" he was brought to me the following day, and though he was a very strong man, I found
his mental disquiet had greatly affected his body.   I
observed that his reason was clear and undisturbed, as
he was able to give a distinct account of himself. He was
impressed with particular sins, and in a lively manner felt
himself to be a guilty condemned sinner. He had a deep
impression of original sin and corruption, as rendering him
liable to eternal wrath, even though he had not been guilty
of actual sin. He had also a deep sense of the hatefulness
of sin, as committed against God, and the sin of unbelief,
as hardening his heart against the voice of Christ, in the
reading or hearing of His Word. He was struck with
dreadful fears of falling into the state of torment, and saw
the great goodness and long suffering of God, in not cut-
ting him off in the midst of his iniquity. He was supported sometimes by views of the remedy, Christ Jesus,
that He had come into the world to save sinners, which he
desired to lay hold of, for the ground of his hope. He
soon attained to some composure of mind, in essaying to
close with Jesus Christ." Conversing with L. M. again,
eight days after, Mr. Robe writes—" He declared that

when engaged in prayer, he felt his soul going out in the acceptance of a whole Christ as his only Saviour; his Prophet to teach him by his Word and Spirit; his Priest to reconcile him to God by his sacrifice; his King to subdue his sin, sanctify, and rule him. He disclaimed all confidence in his duties, and desired to rely on Him alone for salvation; withal, giving himself to the Lord to be saved, upon his own terms, to live unto him, and to serve him in newness of life—resolving also, in the strength of Jesus Christ, to live a holy life to his glory, and yet not to rest on it as a ground of peace and acceptance. He said, he was greatly afraid lest he should fall back unto sin, and be a scandal to religion, after what God had done for him, He was exercised with the fears of hypocrisy and presumption in receiving Christ, against which it relieved him to look unto Christ anew who came to save the chief of sinners, and who is offered to him, in common with all others."

"L. M.," says Mr. Robe, "who was before this blameless in his life, is now spiritual, edifying, and exemplary in his ordinary conversation and deportment."

Cne other instance may be quoted from the narrative of Mr. Robe;—

"After a Sermon preached on the Monday of the Sacrament, by Mr. Webster of Edinburgh, a young woman was brought to Mr. Robe, who found her so filled with a sense of the love of God to her soul, and with love to Jesus Christ, that she was all in tears, and could not refrain from weeping with joy. She had been awakened at Kilsyth about the beginning of July, but had obtained no sensible relief till she heard Mr. Webster. Before her awakening, she was of a blameless life, but when brought to feel the spirituality of God's law, she was filled with alarm on account of the coming wrath. Sometime after, hearing Mr. Webster, she was enabled to state distinctly the consolation she experienced in taking hold of Christ in all his offices. Her subsequent conduct in life was of such a kind as to make it manifest that she was now born from above."

These examples are produced from among the many that might be selected, and furnish decisive evidence that the instructions delivered by the Pastors, and the experience of the people, were of the most scriptural kind; but it may be interesting to state, in Mr. Robe's own

words, what was the doctrine that was so zealously propagated, and which God's Holy Spirit honoured so much :—
" I feared to daub or deal slightly with my people, but told great and small that they were by nature the children of the Devil, while they were in the state of unbelief; and, that if they continued so to the end, I told them, in our Lord's plain terms, they would be damned. I resolved that I would cry aloud, and not spare, and preach with the seriousness and fervour of one that knew that my hearers must either be prevailed with or be damned; and so that they might discern I was in good sadness with them, and really meant as I spoke. Aware that the greater part of every public audience is secure, unconcerned, and fearless, I preached the terrors of the law in the strongest terms I could, that is to say, in express scripture terms. Yet I ever delighted to follow up such statements with a declaration of the gospel of the grace of God. After the law had done its office, I have seen the congregation in tears of joy when the law of grace from Mount Zion was proclaimed." Such statements as these, full of earnestness and faithfulness, and scripture simplicity, joined with believing prayer, are ever accompanied more or less with Divine power, and in the instances now related, were so abundantly blessed, as to make it manifest that they are not the doctrines which man's wisdom teacheth, but which the Holy Ghost teacheth ;—the true sayings of God.

The preaching of the other Ministers was in perfect agreement with this outline, and the very names of many of them are a sufficient guarantee for the soundness of their doctrines.—Mr. M'Laurin Mr. Gillies of Glasgow, Mr. Willison of Dundee, Mr. Bonar of Torphichen, Mr. Whitefield, and many others, were severally engaged in promoting the work, and have severally attested the truth of the facts that have been related. They are still well known to the Church by their able and judicious writings. These men acknowledged that the work was of God. They had the means of examining the experience and character of those who were its subjects. They laboured and prayed that the good work might spread over the land, that it might fill the whole earth. And besides, there is the evidence of Dr. Erskine of Edinburgh, who was ordained in the parish of Kirkintilloch, in the year 1744, and continued there till 1754. During that period he must have had sufficient opportunity of knowing the doctrines that had been preached, and the views and character of those who had been awakened, and he has given his recorded testimony to the reality of this work; and to the fact that the subjects of it in that parish lived as became the followers of the meek and lowly Jesus.—"The memory of the just is blessed." The men who were honoured of God to edify the church during this interesting period of Scottish history, have long since gone the way of all the earth. "They rest from their labours, and their works do follow them." As they that have turned many to righteousness, they now shine as the stars for ever and ever.

It is now nearly a century since the Revival, which has just been related, took place; but the traces of it still remain—many Prayer Meetings exist, and not a few of them in Glasgow, that can date their institution from the period now referred to. The work of the Lord has been going on, though silently, in Scotland ever since. Many have been the faithful pastors that have been instrumental in gathering strayed sheep, in feeding "the flock of God, which He has purchased with his own blood." It is the earnest and increasing prayer of the friends who issue these Tracts, that the number of such faithful men may be greatly increased, that the zeal of church rulers may be extended, that the exertions and prayers of the Christian people may be rendered more abundant, and more fervent; that so the church in this land may be revived, and may yet appear "fair as the moon, clear as the sun, and terrible as an army with banners."

Let every one into whose hand this Tract may come, be assured, that he is by nature dead in trespasses and sins, and that without the experience of the life-giving energy of the Holy Spirit, he must for ever perish. Let him know that there is "a fountain opened for sin and for uncleanness;" let him understand that that fountain is the Redeemer's blood. Let him, without delay, repair to it. Let him "wash and be clean." Then, being freed from the curse of the law, invested with the Redeemer's "robe of righteousness," dwelt in by "the Spirit of promise," he will look abroad over the earth, and earnestly breathe out the simple, yet sublime prayer of the Saviour—"Thy kingdom come. Thy will be done on earth, as it is in heaven."

REVIVALS OF RELIGION.

No IV.

STEWARTON, 1625—SHOTTS, 1630.

THE blessed promise of God to his ancient church, that, ' when the enemy should come in like a flood, the Spirit of the Lord would lift up a standard against him," has often been fulfilled in the experience of the Church of Scotland throughout the many eventful periods of her history. Soon after the death of Knox, attempts were made by the enemies of the truth to overturn that church order and discipline which, under the blessing of God, had been established in this country by the great Reformer; but these attempts were not permitted for the time to be successful. Andrew Melville was raised up to catch as it were the mantle of the departed Reformer, and, like him, in the strength of God, nobly to assert and defend the liberty of the church and her exclusive subjection to her divine Head. Nor was he left to fight the battle alone. Welch of Ayr, the son-in-law of Knox, James Melville, and others who might be named, aided him in contending earnestly for the faith once delivered to the saints. They were eminently men of prayer, as the history of Welch sufficiently testifies, and like the patriarch, had power with God and prevailed; and for a time they were enabled to defeat all the wiles of the adversary, and carry forward the church to a measure of purity and efficiency, beyond what she had formerly attained. This state of things continued with slight interruptions till about the period of the ascension of James to the throne of England, when the church was again brought into the furnace of affliction.

Melville and Welch, for their faithful contending, were first imprisoned, and afterwards banished their native country, while those ministers who were permitted to remain were forbidden to preach, and grievously harassed by the infliction of heavy fines and occasional imprisonment. This state of matters continued till the death of James, and during the early part of the reign of Charles the first. But, though the powers that then were had banished and otherwise removed the ministers, they could not destroy the effects of their labours; for being faithful men, they had been much honoured by the great Head of the church, in the conversion of souls. A spirit of prayer and supplication was poured out upon their bereaved flocks, and they were wonderfully enabled in patience to possess their souls, so that no sufferings, however great, could induce them to abandon those principles which they firmly believed to be the truth and cause of God, neither did they ever give themselves entirely to despair. "Nay," says Guthrie, in his memoirs, in reference to this period, " when the darkness was at the greatest, and when to the eye of reason there seemed scarcely a ray of hope, the Presbyterians declared that utter desolation shall yet be to the haters of the virgin daughter of Scotland. The bride shall yet sing as in the days of her youth. The dry olive tree shall again bud, and the dry dead bones shall live; for the Lord shall prophesy to the dry bones, and the Spirit shall come upon them, and they shall live." " On-waiting," says Rutherford, " has ever a blessed issue; and to keep the word of God's patience, keepeth still the saints dry in the water, cold in the fire, and breathing blood-hot in the grave."

Though their efforts were as yet unavailing to free the Church from the bondage under which she groaned, let it not be imagined that they prayed and fasted altogether in vain. Many faithful ministers, such as Dickson, Livingstone, and Henderson, had great boldness given them to preach the glorious gospel, while standing forward amidst much opposition to witness for the cause of truth. The remarkable revivals which took place at Stewarton, and at the communion at the Kirk of Shotts—narratives of which form the subject of this tract—tended not a little to revive their drooping spirits, and increase their hope and confidence in their heavenly Father, who, having thus "appeared to water his heritage when it was weary," would in his own good time and way work out their complete deliverance. Nor were they disappointed. The deliverance of the Church was ultimately accomplished, and she came out of the furnace purer and fairer than ever—so much so, that the state of the Church after the glorious second Reformation of 1638 is still looked back to as one of the brightest periods of her history.

The awakening at Stewarton having occurred first in the order of time, we shall proceed to give a detailed account of the circumstances connected with it, as they are to be found in the history of those times. The parish of Stewarton, at the period referred to, had for its minister the Rev. Mr. Castlelaw, who appears from the sequel to have had the spiritual welfare of his flock very much at heart; but the principal instrument employed by the great Head of the Church in originating and carrying on this Revival, was the Rev. David Dickson, minister of the neighbouring parish of Irvine.

Mr. Dickson had been formerly Professor of Moral Philosophy in the University of Glasgow; but on receiving a call from the town of Irvine to be their minister, he resigned his chair in the college, and was ordained to the pastoral office in that town in the year 1618. For four years he continued to labour there with great acceptance; but Satan becoming alarmed at the inroads that were making upon his kingdom, through means of Mr. Dickson's ministry, stirred up the persecuting party against him, who summoned him to appear before the High Commission Court at Edinburgh, on the 9th of January, 1622. On his appearance before the court, he was urged to submit to those arbitrary measures they were at this time forcing on the Church. Upon his refusal, he was not only subjected to the most insulting and contemptuous treatment, but sentenced to be ejected from the parish of Irvine, and banished to Turreff, in the north of Scotland, during the pleasure of the court. To all this Mr. Dickson meekly replied, " The will of the Lord be done; though ye cast me off, the Lord will take me up. Send me whither you will, I hope my Master will go with me ; and as he has been with me heretofore, he will be with me still, as being his own weak servant." The Master whom he so dearly loved and so faithfully served having much people in Irvine and its vicinity, who were to be to Him for a name and a praise, did not permit him to remain long in banishment. Having the hearts of all men in his hand, turning them whithersoever he will, He stirred up the Earl of Eglinton, the magistrates and others of the town of Irvine, to petition for his release from the sentence of banishment; and through the overruling providence of God, their request was granted, and about the end of June, 1623, Mr. Dickson was permitted to return to his flock without any condition whatever being imposed upon him.

After his return, his ministry was singularly countenanced and honoured of God for the conviction and conversion of multitudes. Few ministers in his day were more useful in opening up the way of salvation, and leading souls to Christ as their only refuge; so that persons under deep exercise and soul concern came from all the parishes round about Irvine to attend his preaching, and not a few even came from distant parts of the country to settle at Irvine, in order that they

might statedly enjoy the benefit of his ministry. The communion seasons, especially, were times of great refreshing
from the presence of the Lord and the glory of his power.
The enjoyment of such a privilege in other parts of the country
being very rare, caused these seasons at Stewarton to be attended by the most eminent Christians from all corners of the
land; and so great was the power accompanying the preaching of the gospel, that few Sabbaths passed without some
convincing proofs being given of the Holy Spirit's carrying
home the word spoken to the hearts and consciences of the
hearers. Many, who afterwards became solid and lively Christians, were so filled with a sense of the awful evil of sin, and
a view of their own vileness and unworthiness, that they were
quite overpowered, and had to be carried out of the church.

On the Sabbath evenings after sermon, many persons under
soul distress came to Mr. Dickson at his house, with whom
he usually spent an hour or two in hearing their cases, and
in comforting and directing such as were in doubt or despon-
dency. Indeed for this department of his ministerial work
he was remarkably fitted; for his Divine Master had given
him in a very special manner " the tongue of the learned,
that he might know how to speak a word in season to him
that was weary."

Encouraged by these visible tokens of the power of the
blessed Spirit, Mr. Dickson began a weekly lecture on the
Mondays. That being the market day in Irvine, the town
was usually thronged by people from the country; but so
wisely did he arrange the time when the congregation assembled, that the lecture was usually over before the market
began. The people from the parish of Stewarton, especially,
availed themselves of this privilege; and as many of them as
were able to travel, regularly attended Irvine market with
some little commodities for sale, their chief design being to
hear the Monday lecture. To this they were greatly encouraged by their minister, who strongly urged his parishioners
to avail themselves of the privilege of hearing Mr. Dickson,
and their example stirred up others in their own and other
parishes, who also attended; so that the power of religion was
felt throughout that part of the country.

Nor was this all. In a large hall in the manse, there would
often be assembled upwards of a hundred serious Christians,
waiting to converse with him, after the lecture, as to the state
of their souls, and join with him in devotional exercises. And
it was by means of these week-day discourses and meetings
that the famous Stewarton Revival began, and spread after-

wards from house to house for many miles along the valley through which the Stewarton water runs. Many, who had been well known as most abandoned characters, and mockers of every thing bearing the semblance of religion, being drawn by motives of curiosity to attend these lectures, afterwards became completely changed, showing by their life and conversation that the Lord had opened their hearts " to attend unto the things spoken by his servant."

The great enemy of souls, when he found that he could not hinder the progress of this Revival, endeavoured to bring reproach upon it, by leading some who seemed to be under serious concern about their souls into great extravagances, both in the church under sermon, and at private meetings ; but the Lord enabled Mr. Dickson, and others who conversed with them, to act so prudently, that Satan's design was in a great measure frustrated, and solid, serious, practical religion, flourished greatly—illustrating in a remarkable manner what is said of God's ancient people in a similar situation, " That the more they were afflicted, the more they multiplied and grew."

The pious Mr. Robert Blair, who was at this time a professor in the College of Glasgow, often visited Stewarton during the vacation, for the purpose of assisting in the work, and conversing with the people. When there, he resided with the Lady Robertland, a person well known in those times for her piety and the interest she took in the spiritual welfare of others. Mr. Blair preached frequently to the people of Stewarton, and was very useful in assisting in carrying forward the work of revival. Many of the people were at first under great terror and deep exercise of conscience, arising from the views they obtained of the exceeding sinfulness of sin, who afterwards, through the Spirit's teaching, attained to sweet peace and strong consolation by believing in Jesus Christ ; thus illustrating the promise of the Saviour, that when the Spirit would come into the hearts of sinners to make them willing in the day of his power, he would not speak of himself, but take of the things of Christ, and show them to their souls, that looking to the finished work of Christ they might see how completely all the demands of the broken covenant had been met and answered by the blessed Redeemer, and that through this new and living way the chief of sinners may now have access by one Spirit unto the Father, and so be filled with joy and peace in believing.

Mr. Blair modestly observes, " that in these conferences with the people of Stewarton he thought that he profited more by conversing with them, than they did with him." Although formalists and men not knowing the gospel brought against them the charge that was once made against the great apostle of the Gentiles, when he replied, I am not mad, but speak forth the words of truth and soberness—I bless the Lord, says Mr. Blair, that ever I was acquainted with them, and for the help I received by interchanging letters with Mr. Dickson, whereby I was greatly assisted, according to my ability, to relieve them that were in spiritual distress, and to sympathise tenderly with such as I knew to be tempted, and lying under heavy pressure of conscience, so that I still learned more of the wicked wiles of Satan, and of the blessed way of God.

The venerable Principal Boyd of Glasgow, who was at this time living in retirement on his own estate in Carrick, came also to visit this parish; and having conversed with many of the people, he heartily blessed God for the rich display of his mercy towards them, and for the manifestations of his grace in them. Anna, Countess of Eglinton, although bred in her youth amid the splendour of a court, was an humble and eminent Christian, and exerted all her influence for the promotion of the interests of religion. Eglinton Castle being often a shelter for the persecuted ministers of the gospel, she took a deep and lively interest in the work at Stewarton, and persuaded her noble husband to give up for a few days the sports of the field to converse with some of the people she had invited to the castle for that purpose. His lordship declared, after conferring with them, " that he never spoke with the like of them, and wondered at the wisdom they manifested in their conversation."

This great spring-tide of the gospel, says Fleming in his work on the Fulfilling of the Scriptures, did not last for a short time merely, but continued many years—commencing about 1625, and ending about 1630, and, like a spreading stream, increasing as it flows, and fertilizing all within its reach, so did the power of godliness advance from one place to another, increasing in its progress, and throwing a marvellous lustre over those parts of the country. The fame of this Revival brought many from distant parts of the country, who, when they came and witnessed the gladdening sight of so many turned from darkness to light, and walking in the fear of the Lord and comfort of the Holy Ghost, thanked God and took courage, and became more earnest in prayer than ever for the descent of the Spirit on other parts of the Church. The remembrance of the gracious promise, that " for all these things I will be inquired of by the House of

Israel to do it for them," would quicken their importunities at a throne of grace—that God for Christ's sake would come and visit that vine which his own right hand had planted, and make it fruitful and fill the whole land.

This brings us to the Narrative of the Revival at Shotts. This Parish is situated in the Upper Ward of Lanarkshire, and seems to have enjoyed in these troublous times the rare privilege of having a stated minister amongst them disposed to promote the interests of religion. Of his pastoral labours nothing is now known, except in connection with this remarkable Revival. The manse, says Gillies in his Collections, was at this time situated where the public inn now stands, and being far from any place of entertainment, was often resorted to by strangers. Some ladies of rank, who had occasion often to travel that way, received at different times civilities from the minister, particularly on one occasion when their carriage broke down near to the manse, he kindly invited them to alight and remain at his house till it could be repaired, so as to enable them to proceed on their journey. During their stay in the house, they noticed that it had little accommodation, and was much out of repair. In gratitude for his kind attention to them, they got a new manse built for the minister, and in a better situation. Mr. Hance, on receiving so substantial a favour, waited on the ladies to thank them for their kindness, and wished to know if there was any thing in his power he could do to testify his gratitude. The ladies loved the gospel, and the persecuted ministers who were faithfully witnessing for its purity. They therefore gladly seized the opportunity of asking Mr. Hance to invite such of them as they named to assist at the sacrament, in order that they might enjoy the benefit of their ministrations, and also give an opportunity to others to partake of so precious a privilege, at this time rarely enjoyed. To this the minister gladly consented; and information of it spreading abroad, brought together an immense number of choice Christians, from all parts of the country, to attend the dispensation of the ordinance, which was fixed for Sabbath, the 20th June, 1630.

Nothing is now known of the names of the ministers who conducted the preparatory exercises, nor of the subjects to which they directed the attention of the people, but this that the venerable Mr. Robert Bruce was one of their number, and that the Holy Spirit was evidently at work in the hearts of the worshippers, much of their time being spent in social prayer and spiritual conference. Their prayers for the ministers were heard in their own happy experience; for with great power were they enabled to witness of the resurrection of the Lord Jesus, and great grace was upon them all. Much of the Spirit of light and love was imparted on the Sabbath of communion; and so filled were they with joy and peace in believing, that instead of retiring to rest on the evening of the communion Sabbath, they joined together in little companies, and spent the whole of the night in devotional exercises. And there is no doubt that while their hearts were thus filled with the love of Christ, they would be touched with the tenderest pity for the situation of those perishing around them strangers to this love, and that many fervent petitions would be presented in their behalf at a throne of grace.

It had not been usual in those times to have sermon on the Monday after the dispensation of the Lord's supper; but God had given so much of his gracious presence on this occasion, and afforded his people so much communion with himself, on the preceding days, that they knew not how to part on the Monday without thanksgiving and praise. And while their hearts were thus warm with the love of God, some expressed their desire of a sermon on the Monday, and were joined by others, till in a little the desire became general. Mr. John Livingstone, chaplain to the Countess of Wigton, (at that time only a preacher, not an ordained minister, and about twenty-seven years of age,) was with difficulty prevailed on to consent to give the sermon. The night before had been spent by him, and most of the Christians present, in prayer and conference; but when he was alone in the fields in the morning, there came upon him such a misgiving, under a sense of unworthiness and unfitness to speak before so many aged and worthy ministers, and eminent and experienced Christians, that he was thinking of stealing away, and had actually gone to some distance, and was just about to lose sight of the kirk, when these words, " Was I ever a barren wilderness, or a land of darkness?" were brought into his mind with such an overcoming power, as constrained him to think it his duty to return and comply with the call to preach. He accordingly preached, with much assistance, for about an hour and a half, on the points he had meditated, from Ezekiel xxxvi. 25, 26—" Then will I sprinkle clean water upon you, and ye shall be clean : from all your filthiness, and from all your idols, will I cleanse you. A new heart also will I give you, and a new spirit will I put within you; and I will take away the stony heart out of your flesh, and I will give you an heart of flesh."

As he was about to close the discourse, a heavy shower came suddenly on, which made the people hastily take to their cloaks and mantles, and he proceeded to speak to the following purpose :—" If a few drops of rain so discompose you, how discomposed would you be—how full of horror and despair, if God should deal with you as you deserve? and thus he will deal with all the finally impenitent. God might justly rain fire and brimstone upon you, as he did upon Sodom and Gomorrah, and the other cities of the plain. But, for ever blessed be his name! the door of mercy still stands open for such as you are. The Lord Jesus Christ, by tabernacling in our nature, and obeying that law which we have wickedly and wilfully broken, and suffering that punishment we have so richly deserved, has now become a refuge from the storm, and a covert from the tempest of divine wrath, due to us for sin. His merits and mediation are the alone defence from that storm, and none but those who come to Christ just as they are, empty of every thing, and take the offered mercy at his hand, will have the benefit of this shelter." In such expressions, and many others, was he led on for about an hour, (after he had finished what he had premeditated,) in a strain of exhortation and warning, with great enlargement and melting of heart, and with such visible impression on his audience, as made it evident that the power of God was present with them. And, indeed, so great was the power of God manifested on the occasion, that about 500 persons were converted, principally by means of this sermon.

Of this day's exercises Mr. Livingstone has himself left the following memorandum :—" The day in all my life whereiu I found most of the presence of God in preaching, was on a Monday after the communion, in the churchyard of Shotts, June 21, 1630. The night before, I had been in company with some Christians, who spent the night in prayer and conference. When I was alone in the fields in the morning, before the time of sermon, there came such a misgiving of spirit upon me, considering my own unworthiness and weakness, and the multitude and expectation of the people, that I was consulting with myself to have stolen away and declined preaching; but I thought I durst not so distrust God, and so went to sermon, and got good assistance about one hour and a half upon the points which I had meditated on. And in the end, offering to close with some words of exhortation, I was led on about an hour's time in a strain of exhortation and warning, with such liberty and melting of heart, as I never had the like in public all my lifetime. Some little of that stamp remained on the Thursday after, when I preached at Kilmarnock; but the very Monday following, preaching at Irvine, I was so deserted, that the points I had meditated and written, and which I had fully in my memory, I was not able to get pronounced—so it pleased the Lord to counterbalance his dealings, and to hide pride from man."

Of the effects of this work, Mr. Fleming, then minister of Cambuslang, writes—" I can speak on sure grounds, that about five hundred had at that time a discernible change wrought in them, of whom most proved lively Christians. It was the sowing of a seed through Clydesdale, so as many of the most eminent Christians in that country could date either their conversion, or some remarkable confirmation from it: and this was the more remarkable, that one, after much reluctance, by a special and unexpected providence, was called upon to preach that sermon on the Monday, which was not usually practised. And the night before being spent in prayer, the Monday's work might be discerned as a convincing return of prayer."

The following particular instance of the mercy of God on this occasion is well attested:—On that remarkable Monday, three young gentlemen belonging to Glasgow, had made an appointment to go to Edinburgh, to attend the public amusements. Having alighted at Shotts to take breakfast, one of their number proposed to go and hear sermon, probably more from curiosity than any other motive. And for greater expedition, they arranged to come away just at the end of the sermon, before the last prayer. But the power of God was so felt by them, accompanying the sermon, that they could not come away till all was over. When they returned to take their horses, they called for some refreshment before they mounted; but when it was set upon the table, they all looked to one another, none of them daring to touch it till a blessing was asked; and as they were not accustomed formerly to attend to such things, one of them at last remarked, " I think we should ask a blessing." The others assented at once to this proposal, and put it on one of their number to do it, to which he readily consented. And when they had done, they could not rise until another should return thanks. They went on their way more sedately than they used to do, but none of them mentioned their inward concern to the others—only now and then one would say, " Was it not a great sermon we heard?" Another would answer, " I never heard the like of it." They went to Edinburgh: but instead of attending the amusements, they kept their rooms the greater part of the time they were there, which was only about two days, when they were all quite weary of Edinburgh, and proposed to return home. Upon the way home, they did not discover the state of their minds to one another; and after arriving in Glasgow, they kept their rooms very much, coming seldom out. At last one of them made a visit to another, and declared to him what God had done for him at Shotts. The other frankly owned the concern that he had been brought under at the same time; and both of them proceeding to the third, and finding him in the same state of mind, they all three agreed immediately to begin a fellowship meeting. They continued to have a practice suitable to their profession for the remainder of their lives, and became eminently useful in their day and generation.

Another instance, equally well authenticated, is related of a poor man, a coachman in Glasgow, employed by a lady to drive her conveyance to the Shotts. During the sermon, he had taken out his horse to feed at a small distance from the tents; and when the power of God was so much felt during the latter part of the sermon, he apprehended that there was a more than ordinary concern among the people. He felt something strike him in such a way as he could not account for. He hastily rose up and ran into the congregation, where he was made a sharer of what God was distributing among them that day.

The following important testimony to the after life and conversation of many of the persons brought under the power of religion on this remarkable occasion is given by Mr. Andrew Gray of Chryston, an eminently pious old gentleman, in a letter embodied in Gillies' Collection:—

" Notwithstanding the blessed Reformation from Popery, which God brought about by the endeavours of a few, the bulk of the country continued in much ignorance and immorality. But two springs of the revival of religion in this corner, were the famous sermon at the Kirk of Shotts, and the labours of Mr. Robert Bruce. At the sermon at Shotts, a good number of people were by grace made acquainted with the life and power of religion—many of them became eminently good men, and remarkable not only for a pious, inoffensive behaviour, but also for abounding in all the good fruits which pure and undefiled religion enables its sincere followers to perform. Among other good fruits, you cannot doubt a strong inclination to promote the spiritual good of others was a principal one. As the labourers were then few in this part of God's vineyard, he seemed to have inspired these private Christians with an uncommon degree of love to the souls of men—inciting them to labour, by all proper methods, to bring others to the knowledge of that grace which had produced such blessed effects on themselves: and their labours were not without a considerable effect. They were called the Puritans of the Muir of Bothwell, perhaps by way of reproach, by those who were ill affected towards them. Some relations of mine were much the better for having conversed with them. I have seen some of those people myself, who lived to a great age, and have conversed with many good people at this house, who had been very well acquainted with them."

In conclusion, it is very worthy of notice, that, previous to the revival at Shotts, there had been much fervent prayer on the part of the preacher, and prolonged social prayer on the part of the people. And it has been well remarked by a late writer, that while God sometimes works without his people, he never refuses to work with them. Certain it is, that when the hearts of his children are united and enlarged in prayer for a blessing on the ministrations of their pastors, the blessing will not be withheld. God is more ready to give than we are to ask. And it may truly be said, that if we have not now such glorious displays of God's power, it is simply " because we ask not," or asking, we " ask not in faith," forgetting the Saviour's solemn promise, " Verily, verily I say unto you, Whatsoever ye shall ask the Father in my name he will give it you. Hitherto have ye asked nothing in my name: ask and ye shall receive, that your joy may be full."

Reader! are you a stranger to the exercise of believing prayer? Remain not a moment longer, we beseech you, in such an awful condition. Know that to you *now* is the word of salvation sent; and for your encouragement we tell you from the Bible—God so loved the world that he gave his only begotten Son, that whosoever believeth in him should not perish but have everlasting life. This is a faithful saying, and worthy of all acceptation, that Christ Jesus came into the world to save sinners.

REVIVALS OF RELIGION.

No. V.

ISLAND OF ARRAN,

During the years 1804, *&c. but especially in* 1812, 1813.

By the Rev. ANGUS M'MILLAN, Minister of Kilmorie.

THIRTY years ago, the state of religion in this island was exceedingly low. " Darkness covered the land, and gross darkness the people." But, through the tender mercy of God, the day-spring from on high visited it. Divine light arose on them that sat in darkness, and the cause of Christ has gained much ground in this part of his vineyard, since the year 1804. In that year, and the year following, many were awakened at the north end of the island, especially about the farms of Sannox and their neighbourhood. And although this awakening, as to its power and progress, was not of long continuance, yet a considerable number of the subjects of it testified, by their after lives and conversation, that they had undergone a gracious change. This day of small things was the commencement of the revival which followed. From this time, a change for the better might be observed in the religious sentiments and conduct of many among the people. Many seemed now to be awakened from the slumber of spiritual death ; being disposed to attend to the things which belong to their everlasting peace. Their eyes were now opened to see the evil of their former wicked ways, their perishing condition as sinners, and their need of Christ as a Saviour. They now began also to *distinguish* between *truth* and *error ; to relish evangelical doctrine ; to attend with diligence* on the means of grace ; and, in general, *to set up the worship of God, morning and evening, in their families. Religious meetings* were also set up in many places ; and, in the course of a few years, a kind of reformation was thus visible throughout many parts of the island. This was the case more especially, though not exclusively, in the parish of Kilmorie, which was at this time favoured with the ministry of the late pious and laborious **Mr. M'Bride**. It may be remarked, respecting his usual style of preaching, that he was by no means what might be called an alarming preacher, but rather the opposite. His sermons were frequently close and searching ; but he dwelt more on the consolations of the gospel than on the terrors of the law ; and the excitement seemed to be, in general, greater under the sermons in which the riches of divine grace and the con-solations of the gospel were exhibited, than under such as were more awful, and apparently better fitted to awaken. Mr. M'Bride's manner of preaching was very much distinguished for seriousness, fervour, and great zeal for the salvation of sinners ; and this often led him to make very close appeals to the conscience. But the revival itself was not of a sudden. It was gradual, and spread from one place to another. Neither was it in all cases saving as to its effects. Many under it assumed a form of godliness, who were altogether destitute of its power. In other cases, however, there was something more deep and precious—even the quickening, saving, and soul-transforming influence of the Holy Spirit. During its pro-gress, a considerable number were accordingly brought under deep convictions of their guilt and unworthiness as sinners, of their liability to eternal misery, and of their utter help-lessness as concerned themselves. Now, they began in earnest to say, " What shall we do to be saved ?"—and to count all things but loss for the excellency of the knowledge of Christ Jesus ; for an interest in him. And the God of all grace, who thus visited them with the awakening influences of his Spirit, was pleased also to enlighten their minds as to the way of sal-vation ; and thus to lead them by faith for peace and rest to the only Saviour of sinners. And being thus quickened, enlight-ened, and comforted, by the teaching of the same Spirit, they were also united together in the bonds of love and Christian fellowship, while they travelled together Zionward.

The subjects of these spiritual influences were, however, only as a little flock, when compared with the multitude who remained yet stout-hearted and far from righteousness. And these, becoming impatient under the restraints which the late reformation had laid upon them, with regard to unholy prac-tices, began to break out anew with greater violence ; so that, in 1810 and 1811, many were bolder in sin, and more aban-doned to wickedness, than they had been at any former period. The enemy of souls now came in as a flood and threatened to carry all before him. It is right, however, to observe, that this was in no respect true of professors, or of such as there was reason to believe had been the subjects of divine grace. These were for the most part remarkably consistent in their walk and conversation. The breaking out of sin, here referred to, was among the bulk of the people, who made no particular profession of religion, and especially among the young, who had been brought under temporary restraint.

These circumstances, however, affected the tender-hearted, and stirred up the pious zeal of Mr. M'Bride, and led him to be even more earnest in his warnings and remonstrances from the pulpit, and otherwise, against abounding iniquity. The little flock of tender hearted Christians, scattered throughout his parish, were, at the same time, moved with a sense of the prevalence of sin, and the desolations of Zion. They felt an increased concern for the conversion and salvation of sinners, and a deeper interest in the prosperity and enlargement of the kingdom of Christ. They began to be more frequent and earnest in their supplications at a throne of grace for a time of revival—of refreshing from the presence of the Lord. Several little parties of them by mutual consent, set apart some days for private fasting and prayer, sending up their united supplications to the Hearer of prayer, for the down-pouring of the Spirit in his awakening and converting influences on sinners around them. They kept several such days *for nearly a twelve-month* before the commencement of what is generally called, "The Revival of Religion in Arran." In these devotional exercises, some of them enjoyed uncommon nearness to God, and great freedom at a throne of grace, when pouring out their hearts, in earnest supplication, for the manifestation of divine power and glory in the sanctuary, especially in the congregation with which they were themselves connected. Their minds were much stirred up to press after these things in secret, and at their fellowship meetings, and also when attending public ordinances. They seemed to be animated by the spirit of him who said, "For Zion's sake I will not hold my peace, and for Jerusalem's sake I will not rest, until the righteousness thereof go forth as brightness, and the salvation thereof as a lamp that burneth."

While this little flock of Christ, and their pastor at their head, were thus engaged, and about the beginning of March, 1812, the Lord began to work in an unusual way among them, in a way of which they had not till this time any expectation, and which, accordingly, caused some surprise. It was at this time that the outcrying commenced, which was afterwards so common for a considerable time. It began at first in some private meetings, but afterwards extended to the public assembly under Mr. M'Bride's ministry. What made the thing the more remarkable was, *that it made its first appearance among the people of God.* Yea, the most tender, humble, and spiritual minded among them, were the first affected in this manner, and it continued for a short time among them only. But the influence which appeared first moving on them, in this unusual way, was soon extended to others; and the next subjects of it were those who had been before seriously disposed, or who had been at one time or other under serious impressions. But, soon after, it was extended to the gay and thoughtless, the moral, and the openly wicked. Persons of almost every description and age, from nine years or under, to that of sixty or upwards, were affected; but the number of old people was small compared with that of the young. The crying at first, and while confined to the people of God, was attended with very little bodily agitation; but after others were affected, it was generally attended with these—such as panting, trembling, and other convulsive appearances.

The writer of these pages did not reside in Arran till about six months after the commencement of this revival; but he inquired particularly concerning the beginning of it, from such as were best able to inform him, and is satisfied, in his own mind, that the Spirit of the Lord was at work in preparing for it—that his mighty power was revealed in the commencement of it—and that he had a gracious and merciful design in ordering the circumstances of it. Although this revival did in some measure degenerate latterly through the weakness and folly of men, yet the beginning of it was truly the doing of the Lord, and marvellous in our eyes. Some, who were among the first affected, told the writer, that they had not the most remote idea of crying out, before they were constrained to do so. So much was this the case, that they said they could not have refrained, even if they had been threatened with instant death. They added, that their out-cryings and bodily agitations *arose entirely from the state of their minds,* when powerfully impressed and affected with a sense of divine truth. But it is proper to observe, that the writer is here speaking only of such as were lively exercised Christians previous to this revival. On examining others, who knew nothing of Christian experience before the beginning of this work, he found that the first impressions of many of them were accompanied with deep convictions of sin, with a painful sense of their helplessness and misery as sinners, and also with earnest desires after an interest in Christ; which it is to be hoped.many of them attained. But it must be acknowledged, that the accounts given by all were not alike satisfactory. Many were deeply affected externally, who could give little account of the matter. Their affections'were moved, but convictions of sin did not take any deep hold on their hearts and consciences, and so their awakenings soon passed away; at least, it was so with some. But if there be joy in heaven over even one sinner that repenteth, we have reason to think that there must have been much joy, in that world of light and love, over many that were brought to true repentance, in this place, during the progress of that work.

About the beginning of 1812, the awakening became general, and continued to make progress about three months. After this, it seemed to be at a stand, till the beginning of the following December, when it again revived, and continued to spread considerably for about three months more; during which period it extended over a great part of the parish of Kilmorie, which is nearly thirty miles long, and it extended also to some parts of the parish of Kilbride. The writer cannot pretend to give the exact number of the subjects of this awakening; but the number, from first to last, was very considerable. It must have amounted to two or three hundred persons, old and young taken together. He may state them at two hundred and fifty; which is rather below than above the real number. But he does not mean to insinuate that the whole of these proved true believers. This will appear from the statements already made.

For some months after the commencement of the awakening, the subjects of it manifested an uncommon thirst after the means of grace. Both old and young flocked in multitudes to hear the word of God. His house, and the place employed for private meetings, were frequently so crowded, that the people, as it were, trod one on another. To travel ten or fifteen miles to hear sermon, was considered as a very small matter; and after sermon was over, it was no uncommon thing for many of them to meet together in private houses, or in barns, and to spend several hours in religious exercises. Some of them spent even whole nights in this way. They also longed for the return of the Sabbath. They rejoiced when it was said unto them, " Let us go into the house of the Lord." They eagerly sought after renewed opportunities of receiving spiritual instruction. Their desire was so great as not to be easily satisfied. In our religious assemblies, at this time, some might be seen filled with divine love, others with fear; some rejoicing in hope of the glory of God, and others trembling lest they should come short of it; some crying out in accents of praise, and others indicating, by their cries, their dread of everlasting wrath. At this time, our meetings were frequent, and well attended; and almost every sermon seemed to be effective in awakening, quickening, or refreshing. Satan and his agents, indeed, made strong efforts to counteract the designs and operations of the Spirit of God, by throwing all manner of stumblingblocks in the way of his people; but, notwithstanding all the opposition of earth and hell, the word of the Lord grew and multiplied. Some who were lively Christians before, enjoyed at this time much of the refreshing influences of the Spirit, and were often filled, in an extraordinary measure, with peace and joy in believing. As illustrative of this, I may mention, that, in the spring of 1813, I was catechising one day at a particular farm, in the district of ———, and when speaking of the character of Christ as the Redeemer of God's elect, and attempting to describe the preciousness of his blood, and the riches of his grace, an excellent Christian, who is now in the world of spirits, cried out, in an elevated tone of voice, " O the infinite virtue of the blood of Christ—the preciousness of his blood! What am I, what am I, that he should ever spend one thought concerning me! O my nothingness, my nothingness, my nothingness !" And, soon after, she exclaimed, " I shall soon be with thee, I shall soon be with thee—be for ever with the Lord !" I have seen others, also, on various occasions, affected much in the same way. And these ecstasies of spiritual joy, among the people of God, were generally *accompanied with great humility and tenderness of spirit*. Instead of being puffed up, they were, on the contrary, bowed down to the very dust, under a sense of their privileges. When the glory of the King of Zion was manifested to their souls, in the light of the Spirit, they were ready to exclaim, with Job, " Wherefore I abhor myself, and repent in dust and ashes." I have heard others, under awakenings of conscience, cry out, " O what shall we do? what shall we do? Wash us from sin; let us not deceive ourselves, for we cannot deceive thee." It was pleasing thus to see many of them really afraid of self-deception, and earnest in their inquiries after the only sure foundation, the only hope set before them in the Gospel.

In the spring of 1813, this awakening, however, began to decline, and ceased very soon after; but those who were truly Christians, continued to enjoy, both in secret duties and at public ordinances, renewed and manifest tokens of the divine presence and favour. This was especially the case on sacramental occasions; at which they were favoured with the assistance of some of the most pious ministers of the day. Most of these having now departed this life, I am enabled to name the greater part of them, without making any reference to the living. The late Rev. Messrs. Bayne of Greenock, and Robertson of Kingussie, formerly of the Chapel at Rothsay, assisted here constantly for many years. The late Rev. Dr. Love of Anderston assisted here occasionally, about the time of the revival; and the late Rev. Mr. M'Kenzie of Gorbals, formerly of the Gaelic Chapel, Duke Street, Glasgow, assisted also occasionally, but chiefly before the commencement of this work. These, along with the late Mr. M'Bride himself, were considered, and I believe justly, among the most pious ministers of their day: but they have ceased from their labours, and their works do follow them. The more regular or occasional labours of these men, were often blessed as seasons of refreshing from the presence of the Lord. It is doubtless true, that, as the awakening declined, some of those who appeared at one time much affected, and much engaged in religious pursuits, began to grow cold and remiss in spiritual duties, to fall into divers temptations, and to slide back into conformity with the world. Like the stony-ground hearers, the religious impressions of many were slight and transitory —their convictions were not of a spiritual or abiding nature: and, having no root in their hearts, they soon withered away, without bringing forward any fruit to perfection. But although many did thus turn, as the dog to his vomit, and soon got rid of their religious impressions, a considerable number of the subjects of this work continue, to the present day, bringing forth fruit meet for repentance, and manifesting their faith by their works. It is due, however, to acknowledge, that, even in respect of the best of us, the zeal, fervour, and liveliness, manifest during the time of our revival, have suffered some decay; and that, instead of these, coldness, deadness, and formality in religion, are now too prevalent among us. We have, therefore, much need to be earnest in our supplications for another season of refreshing from the presence of the Lord—to pray, with the devout Psalmist —" Turn us, O God of our salvation, and cause thine anger toward us to cease.— Wilt thou not revive us again, that thy people may rejoice in thee? Show us thy mercy, O Lord, and grant us thy salvation."

THE above narrative of what is usually called 'the Arran Revival,' was drawn up by the Rev. A. M'MILLAN, Minister of the Parish of Kilmorie, during the summer of 1830. This was done at the request of the *Glasgow Evangelical Corresponding Society;* for which the undersigned acted, at that time, as Secretary; and it is now published with permission from the Author. We are persuaded, that the pious reader will feel not a little indebted to Mr. M'Millan, for the pains he has taken in detailing and discriminating the facts here narrated. And such as either know him personally, or have taken the trouble of inquiring about him, will not fail to put the fullest confidence in all his statements, as literally and exactly true. These are circumstances of much importance, in a matter of this kind, as it is not so much opinion, however judicious, which enhances such a document, as its being a simple and faithful narration of facts. And being fully satisfied as to this, we very willingly commend the whole to the prayerful consideration of the Lord's people.

D. MACFARLAN.

RENFREW MANSE, *Jan.* 29*th,* 1834.

REVIVALS OF RELIGION.

No. VI.

MOULIN, 1798—1800.

Extracted from a LETTER *by the* REV. ALEXANDER STEWART, *lat Minister of the Parish of Moulin, afterwards of Canongate, Edin burgh, to the* REV. DAVID BLACK, *Minister of Lady Yester's Church, Edinburgh.*

MOULIN, 1*st September*, 1800.

MY DEAR SIR,

As you have signified to me the opinion of Dr. Erskine, Dr. Hunter, and other respected friends, that the happy revival of religion amongst us ought to be more generally known, and that it might be useful to publish an account of it, I shall now endeavour to give a circumstantial detail of its commencement and progress. I am able to do this with tolerable correctness, as my memory is assisted by written notes. I have no doubt that the concern about religion, which has been lately awakened in this place, is already the ground of much rejoicing among the angels before the throne. Pity it should not also engage, as extensively as may be, the praises of our Christian brethren on earth.

The inhabitants of the Highlands have, as you know, the Scriptures in Gælic, their native tongue: the New Testament, the book of Psalms, and the Assembly's Shorter Catechism, have been long read in the schools. By these means, the people in this part of the country had some knowledge of the principal events in the history of the creation and fall of man, and of our Saviour's life, death, resurrection, and ascension; they knew also some of the great outlines of Christian doctrine; but, in general, their knowledge of the principles of Christianity was superficial and confused, and their religious opinions were in many important points erroneous. Very few, indeed, knew the way in which the gospel informs us a sinner may be reconciled to God. The opinion of their own works recommending them to the favour of God, and procuring them a reward from his bounty, was almost universal. It discovered itself in their ordinary speech, in their common remarks on more solemn occasions, and in almost every religious sentiment that was uttered. Their apprehensions of the demerit and consequences of sin were exceedingly defective. I have heard many on a sick bed, after acknowledging, in common form, that they were sinners, deny that they ever did any ill. And in the view of death, they have derived their hopes of future happiness from the reflection, that they had never wronged any person. Very few seemed to annex any meaning to their words, when they said that they expected pardon for Christ's sake. Being without the true knowledge of God, of Christ, of the gospel, of their own character and state, they lived, as might be expected, to themselves and to the world. They were not, indeed, addicted to open vice, if we except lying and swearing. They were rather distinguished for sobriety, industry, and peaceable behaviour. But they were destitute of religious principle. They attended church, and partook of the sacrament, and rested from their work on the Sabbath. But these outward observances were almost the only appearance of religion. There was little reading of the Scriptures at home; little religious instruction of children; hardly any family worship; no religious conversation; no labouring, in any manner, for the meat which endureth unto everlasting life. Even on the Lord's day, most of the time was spent in loitering, visiting, and worldly talk; and on other days religion was scarcely thought of.

In narrating the means by which the people were brought to pay a more serious attention to their eternal interests, it is necessary to say something of my own case. I was settled minister of this parish in 1786, at the age of twenty-two. Although I was not a "despiser" of what was sacred, yet I felt nothing of the power of religion on my soul. I had no relish for its exercises, nor any enjoyment in the duties of my office, public or private. A regard to character, and the desire of being acceptable to my people, if not the only motives, were certainly the principal motives, that prompted me to any measure of diligence or exertion. My public addresses and prayers were, for the most part, cold and formal. They were little regarded by the hearers at the time, and as little recollected afterwards. I preached against particular vices, and inculcated particular virtues. But I had no notion of the necessity of a radical change of principle; for I had not learned to know the import of those assertions of Scripture, that "the carnal mind is enmity against God;" "that if any man be in Christ, he is a new creature;" and, that "except a man be born of water and of the Spirit, he cannot enter into the kingdom of God." I spoke of making the fruit good; but I was not aware that the tree was corrupt, and must first be itself made good, before it could bear good fruit. The people, however, were satisfied with what they heard, and neither they nor I looked farther.

If there were any persons in the parish at the time who lived a life of faith, under the influence of pure, evangelical principles, I did not know them, nor was I qualified to discern and understand what spirit they were of. I have since had reason to believe that there were a very few spiritually-minded persons; but their life was hid, and they had left this world, all but one or two, before they could acknowledge me as a brother.

While I was yet ignorant of the truth, and unacquainted with Christian experience, two persons, under conviction of sin and terrors of conscience, applied to me for advice. They supposed that one in the office of the ministry must, of course, be a man of God, and skilled in administering remedies for the diseases of the soul. They were widely mistaken in their judgment of me; for I had learned less of the practice than of the theory of pastoral duty. I said something to them in the way of advice; but it afforded them no relief. They were, however, under the care of the good Physician. He applied his own balm to their wounded spirits, and "healed, and bade them live." Being progressively and effectually taught of God, they are both now established, judicious Christians. These are the first that appear to have been converted since my incumbency; but they cannot be reckoned the fruits of my ministry.

The Lord was now preparing to gather to himself a fuller harvest in this place. He might have removed me, as a useless encumbrance, or rather an intervening obstacle, out of the way, and subjected me to the doom of the unprofitable servant; but he was graciously pleased to spare me, and visit me in mercy, and even to employ me as one of his instruments in carrying on his own work. Glory to his name who commanded light to shine out of darkness!

The writings of pious men, which were put into my hands by one or another Christian friend, were made the means of bringing me acquainted with the truths of the gospel. Among these, I may mention the works of the Rev. John Newton and Thomas Scott, as eminently useful to me. I was slow in receiving and embracing the doctrines maintained by these writers. By degrees, however, I was persuaded that they were agreeable to Scripture, and that no doubt they must be admitted as true. I therefore durst not preach any thing which I conceived to be directly contrary to these doctrines; but I brought them forward rarely, incorrectly, and with awkward hesitation. The trumpet was sounded, but it gave an " uncertain sound."

The biographical sketches in the Evangelical Magazine were principal means of impressing my heart, of opening my eyes to perceive the truth, of exciting a love to godliness, and a desire after usefulness. The conversation and example of some persons of a truly spiritual mind, to whose acquaintance I was admitted, and who exhibited to my view what I found only described in written memoirs, conduced also much to impress on my mind the truths with which I was gradually becoming more acquainted. I cannot omit mentioning, in this connection, the blessings I enjoyed in the preaching, the prayers, and the conversation, of that much favoured servant of Christ, the Rev. Charles Simeon, of King's College, Cambridge. He was a man sent from God to me; was my guest for two days in June 1796, preached in my church, and left a savour of the things of God, which has remained with us ever since.

From that time, I began to teach and to preach Jesus Christ with some degree of knowledge and confidence. From August 1797, to January 1798, I preached a course of sermons on the fundamental doctrines of Christianity, following, for the most part, the selection and order of texts in the tract entitled, " Short Sermons."

The novelty of the matter, and some change in the manner of preaching, excited attention. People began to think more, and sometimes to talk together, of religious subjects, and of the sermons they heard. But I did not yet know of any deep or lasting impressions having been made. The two persons before mentioned as earliest converted, had by this time got clearer views of the gospel, were enabled to derive comfort from the word of salvation, and began to bear their testimony to the grace of God their

Saviour. They were in use occasionally of visiting a poor infirm woman, who had long walked with God, and who now lived alone in a mean cottage in the neighbouring village. It was proposed that they should come together to her house at a time appointed, and that I and some of my family should join them, and spend an evening hour or two in reading, conversation and prayer. In process of time, different persons, who were enquiring after the one thing needful, hearing how we were employed, and believing that God was with us, were, at their own request, admitted of our party. In this poor woman's little smoky hovel, we continued to hold our weekly meetings to August 1799, when she was called away to join the general assembly of the first-born above. Her growth in grace had been very conspicuous, and her death was triumphant.

In summer, 1798, the Lord's supper was dispensed in our congregation, at the usual time of the year. For some weeks before, I endeavoured, in preaching, to explain more fully, and with more application to the conscience, the nature of the ordinance, and the character of those who, under the denomination of disciples, were commanded to keep it. The exhortations and warnings then given appeared to be accompanied with a divine blessing. Some of the ordinary communicants, judging themselves to be in an unconverted state, kept back of their own accord from partaking of the sacrament. Others, after conversing with me privately on the subject, took the same resolution. And many of those who might otherwise have applied for admission, forbore to apply, there being a much smaller number of applicants than in previous years.

Although the number of communicants was thus for the time diminished, yet the number of those who were brought under concern about their eternal interests was increasing. This concern showed itself chiefly among the younger people under twenty-five or thirty. Their knowledge wa yet imperfect. A natural shyness often hindered them long from discovering to others what they thought or felt. They had as yet no friend or intimate whom they judged able, from experience, to understand their situation, or to give them counsel. Some of them began to visit one or the two earlier converts formerly mentioned, from whose reading and conversation they derived considerable benefit. By means of this common friend, they were brought more acouainted with each other. One might now observe at church, after divine service, two or three small groups forming themselves round our few more advanced believers, and withdrawing from the crowd into the adjacent fields, to exchange Christian salutations, and hold Christian converse together; while a little cousin, or other young relative, followed as a silent attendant on the party, and listened earnestly to their religious discourse.

As the sacrament of the Lord's supper had been much abused, by admitting, without strict examination or special instruction, all candidates who could give a tolerable answer to common questions, and who were free from grosser immoralities, so it must be confessed that the sacrament of baptism had been still more profaned. Nothing but one kind of scandal was understood to preclude a man from admission to this ordinance. Gross ignorance or immoral behaviour, only laid a man open to some admonition or reproof, or, at most, laid him under the necessity of procuring another sponsor, but hardly ever hindered the baptism of his child. Nothing subjects a man to greater disgrace and obloquy among us, than to have his child remain unbaptized. The dominion of custom in this matter is so despotic, that most parents would choose rather to carry their children a hundred miles to be baptized by a popish priest, than to be refused baptism when they demand it. The superstitious notions, and other abuses, attending our celebration of this sacrament, called loudly for reformation. Last year, I preached a short course of sermons on baptism; at the same time, agreeably to a recent resolution and recommendation of the presbytery to which I belong, I revived the laws of the church, which had fallen into disuse, relative to this ordinance, particularly that which prohibits private baptism.

In February, 1799, it pleased God to call home my dear wife, after we had been married little more than five years. She, too, had been growing in grace during the last two years of her life. She laboured for some months under a gradual decline, which impaired her strength, and occasioned sometimes a languor of spirits; but her faith and trust in her Redeemer were, on the whole, uniform and steady. Her dismission from the body was gentle, without pain or struggle. Her meek and humble behaviour, her growing love to her Saviour, and the joy she expressed at the prospect of being soon with him, were blessed to the edification of our pious neighbours, who often called to visit her.

The following month, March, 1799, I began a course of practical sermons on Regeneration, which I continued to the beginning of July following. These were attended with a more general awakening than had yet appeared among us. Seldom a week passed in which we did not see or hear of one, two, or three persons, brought under deep concern about their souls, accompanied with strong convictions of sin, and earnest inquiry after a Saviour. It was a great advantage to these that there were others on the road before them; for they were seldom at a loss now to find an acquaintance to whom they could freely communicate their anxious thoughts. The house of one of our most established Christians became the chief resort of all who wished to spend an hour in reading or conversing about spiritual subjects. Some who had but newly begun to entertain serious thoughts about religion, and who had not yet come so far as to speak out their mind, would contrive an errand to this person's house, and listen to her talk. She was visited at other times by those who were drawn only by curiosity or a disputatious spirit, who wanted to cavil at her words, or draw her into controversy. Such visitors she did not avoid, and at last they ceased to visit her.

Other experienced Christians among us have been extremely useful to their younger brethren or sisters. Their conversation and example have been principal means of turning the attention of the young to religion, and of edifying those who have been already awakened. Such persons I find most serviceable auxiliaries. If they be neither *prophets*, nor *apostles*, nor *teachers*, yet their usefulness in the church entitles them to the appellation of *helps:* 1 Cor. xii, 28. Nor do I think an apostle would hesitate to acknowledge them, both men and women, in the relation of *fellow-labourers:* Phil. iv, 3. Nor has success in this divine work been confined to instruments raised up among ourselves. The same happy effects have, in a certain measure, attended the preaching, the prayers, or conversation, of pious brethren, who have assisted at the celebration of the Lord's supper, or made us other occasional visits.

It is observable that the work of conversion has been begun and carried on among this people in a quiet manner, without any confusion, and without those ungovernable agitations of mind, or convulsions of the body, or shrieking or fainting, which have often accompanied a general awakening in other places. One young woman was so much moved in church, in March, 1799, that she wept bitterly, and her friends thought it prudent to convey her out a little before the congregation was dismissed. She was for five or six days unfit for going about her usual work. In June following, at the time of our sacrament, she felt emotions of joy, for a few days, to such a degree as to withdraw her regard in a great measure from sensible objects. Spiritual affections were unusually strong in her, and spiritual objects appeared visible and near; but her sentiments were quite correct and scriptural. A few days afterwards, when her emotions had subsided, she told me that she was at the time sensible that her mind was somewhat unsettled, but that she found comfort in recollecting the apostle's words, " If we are beside ourselves, it is to God." This was exactly her case. She continues an humble, lively Christian, and, except these two short intervals, she has regularly performed her ordinary work as a maid-servant, to the satisfaction of her master and mistress, in whose service she still remains. Another woman, the mother of a family, in April last, was so much moved in hearing sermon, that of her own accord she left the church. Excepting these two instances, I know of none whose emotions, under the preaching of the Word, discovered themselves in any other manner than by silent tears.

Having lately made an enumeration of those of our congregation, whom, to the best of my judgment, I trust I can reckon truly enlightened with the saving knowledge of Christ, I find their number about seventy. The greater part of these are under thirty years of age; several are above forty; six or seven above fifty; one sixty-six; and one above seventy. Of children, under twelve or fourteen, there are a good many who seem to have a liking to religion; but we find it difficult to form a decided opinion of their case. Of persons who have died within these twelve months, three we are persuaded, and we hope two or three others, have slept in Jesus.

A very considerable number are friendly to religion, and countenance and defend the truth, even while they do not as yet appear to live under its power. A few among ourselves did for a while jeer and deride the godly; but such persons are left in so very small a minority, that they have ceased to be troublesome. The Scriptures, too, are so generally read and referred to, that the truth itself serves to stop the mouth of scoffers. We are sometimes told that

the sentiments and language of our people are much mis-
represented, and are the objects of much wonder, and ridicule, and invective, in other places. But we only hear of
such things; they are hardly permitted to come nigh us.
The chief opposition arises from those who possess superior
scholarship and acquaintance with the Scriptures. These
contend that there can be nothing substantial or necessary
in that experimental knowledge which illiterate persons
may pretend to have attained; and that it is mere ignorance in them to imagine that they can have a larger share
of saving knowledge than men who are greater scholars and
better versed in the Scriptures. " Are we blind also?"
has ever been the indignant language of carnal wisdom, of
literary pride, and of self-righteous presumption.

It is evident that the Scriptures represent all mankind
as divided into two classes. These are distinguished from
each other in the most explicit manner; and the distinction
is marked by the strongest language, and the most significant comparisons. They are called the children of God,
and the children of the devil, (1 John iii, 10); the children of the kingdom, and the children of the wicked one,
(Matt. xiii, 38); the just and the wicked, (Matt. xiii, 49);
they who are dead in trespasses and sins, and they who are
quickened together with Christ, (Eph. ii, 1—6). They
are compared to wheat and tares, (Matt. xiii, 25); to good
and bad fishes, (Matt. xiii, 47, 48); to sheep and goats,
(Matt. xxv, 32). In the general tenor of my preaching,
especially in discussing the important doctrine of regeneration, I have endeavoured to keep in view this distinction,
and to exhibit it clearly to the notice of my hearers.
Many have been not a little offended at such a discrimina-
tion; have found fault with the preacher; have complained
of uncharitable judgment; pleading that it was God's pre-
rogative to judge the heart; that they hoped theirs was
good, though they did not make such a parading profession
of religion, &c. The truth has prevailed, however; and
some have confessed to me, that their first serious thoughts
about the state of their souls, arose from the surprise and
resentment they felt on being classed under the character
of unbelievers, along with murderers and idolaters : Rev.
xxi, 8. But in giving such offensive, though necessary
warnings, I had much need of the spirit of Christ, to repress
all asperity of language and manner, to awaken tender
compassion for those whom I addressed, and to enable me
to speak the truth in love.

I observe among our young converts a considerable
variety of frames, but a striking uniformity of character
They are dejected or elevated, according as their regard is
more fixed on their own deficiencies and corruptions, or on
the glorious sufficiency of Christ. But all of them are
characterised by lowliness of mind, by a warm attachment
to each other, and to all who love the Lord Jesus, and by
the affections set on things above. I know no instances
among them of persons trusting for comfort or direction to
dreams or visions, impulses or impressions: and hardly an
instance of seeking comfort from external signs or tokens,
arbitrarily assumed by the inquirer, after the example
of Abraham's servant, (Gen. xxiv, 14), and of Gideon,
(Judges vi, 36—40).

We have not yet to lament any great falling off in those
who appeared to have once undergone a saving change.
There may be persons who were for a time enquiring, with
some apparent earnestness, and afterwards fell back to their
former unconcern. I have reason to suspect that there
may be several in this situation, though I have not access
to know the exact state of their minds. May the Lord
discover it to themselves in time! But all, so far as I
know, who seemed to have been once truly humbled for
their sins, and made to feel in their hearts the grace of
God in the gospel, continue thus far to maintain an humble, spiritual, conscientious walk. They have a constant
appetite for the sincere milk of the word, and for Christian fellowship with one another. The younger sort have
lost their former levity of speech and behaviour, and are
become devout and sober-minded; those more advanced
in life have laid aside their selfishness and worldly-minded-
ness, and are grown humble, contented, and thankful.

The external effects of a general concern about religion,
have appeared in the behaviour even of those who do not
seem to have experienced a change of heart. While the
younger people attended a Sabbath school, those who
were grown up, used to spend the evening of that day in
sauntering about the fields and woods in gossiping parties, or visiting their acquaintance at a distance, without
improving their time by any profitable exercise. Now,
there is hardly a lounger to be seen, nor any person walking abroad, except going to some house, or meeting, where
he may hear the Scriptures read. Swearing, profane talking, foolish and indecent jesting, have in a great measure

ceased. At late wakes, where people assemble to watch by the body of a deceased neighbour, the whole night used to be spent in childish, noisy sports and pastimes. Even the apartment where the corpse lay was the scene of their revelry. This unnatural custom, which is still pretty general over a great part of the Highlands, is almost wholly discontinued in this part of the country. They still assemble on such occasions; but they pass the time in reading the Bible, or some religious book, and in sober conversation.

I have mentioned, that almost all our converts have been brought to serious concern and inquiry, in a quiet, gradual manner. To an intelligent observer, the change in the conversation, temper, deportment, and the very countenance of individuals, is striking; the change, too, on the general aspect of the manners of the people, is conspicuous. The effect is thus, on the whole, obvious; yet there are few particulars in the case of each person, which, taken singly, will appear uncommon. We have no instances of persons remarkable for profligacy of manners, or profaneness of speech, who have been reclaimed from such enormities; because there were none of that description to be found in our society. The change has been from ignorance and indifference, and disrelish of divine things, to knowledge, and concern, and spiritual enjoyment. Neither are there among us examples of persons suddenly struck and impressed by some alarming event, or singular interposition of Providence. The word of truth, proclaimed in public, or spoken in private, has been almost the only outward means of producing conviction of sin, and confidence in the Saviour. In every single case, the power of God is visible in the effect produced; but there is little " diversity of operation." Instead of endeavouring to paint the beauties of holiness in the scene around me, I rather wish to prevail with you and other friends, who know how to enjoy such a spectacle, to " come and see."

We still have the happiness to find, from week to week, that the same concern and awakening is spreading around, and extending to some neighbouring congregations. Within these few weeks, persons from six or seven miles distance, have called here on a Sabbath morning, under evident concern about their souls. On a succeeding Sabbath, the same persons have called again, introducing a relation, or fellow-servant, under similar concern. All of these, so far as can be judged from present appearances, are in a hopeful way. Such is the manifold grace and loving-kindness with which it has pleased the Lord to visit this corner of his vineyard. I trust that all our Christian brethren, who may receive the joyful intelligence, will join us in praying, that God may continue to water, with showers of blessings, " this vine which his own right hand hath planted;" and that no boar from the wood may be allowed to waste it, nor worm at the root to smite it that it wither. I am, &c.

In the preceding most interesting narrative, as in others of a similar kind, the connection between the PRAYERS of the people of God, and the remarkable visitation of mercy recorded, is one of the most striking features. Mr. STEW-ART had known the truth in its power, and preached it for a considerable time before it was attended with any visible success; and it is not till he has informed us of his weekly meetings for prayer, with three pious persons in the parish, that he proceeds to give an account of the general awakening which followed. Thus it ever has been, and will continue to be. Them that honour God in prayer, he will honour with his blessing. Let those, then, who now desire to see " times of refreshing," such as were experienced at Moulin, be stirred up to imitate the example of these three humble, but Christian individuals, who, in " a mean and smoky hovel," assembled from week to week, with their minister, to supplicate the blessing of the Spirit, and who, doubtless, in secret, poured out many a fervent "breathing" into the bosom of their gracious and loving Father, on behalf of their ungodly neighbours. And praying in the Spirit, they may expect to be favoured with similar results. God will not turn away their prayer. The present is a season when there is a peculiar call to prayer, and when these encouraging words in the Prophecy of Hosea should be engraven on every heart, and their spirit infused into every soul,—" IT IS TIME TO SEEK THE LORD, TILL HE COMB AND RAIN RIGHTEOUSNESS UPON YOU."

REVIVALS OF RELIGION.

THE success of the Reformation from the first was much slower in Ireland than in either of the sister kingdoms. Few Protestant ministers were settled in the country, and these for the most part very ill qualified for the discharge of their duties ; while the government, bent upon a favourite scheme of discontinuing the native Irish language, prohibited its use in the service of the church—permitted no books to be printed in that language, and even directed that in those parishes where the English was not understood by the readers, the church service should be conducted in Latin. With means so exceedingly inadequate it is not surprising that few of the people should have embraced the reformed doctrines, and that the country should have continued essentially Popish.

The province of Ulster, in the early period of the reformation, was in a condition still worse than the other parts of the country. Those intestine wars which raged during the latter part of the reign of Elizabeth had their chief seat here, and had reduced the province almost to a state of depopulation : most of the towns were destroyed ; cultivation had nearly ceased ; and the few proprietors who remained, supported themselves on plunder, and lived in a condition little better than barbarism. In circumstances so very unfavourable the spread of Protestant principles could hardly be otherwise than small, and in fact they were scarcely known beyond a few of the principal towns, insomuch that in the beginning of the reign of James I., Du Pin, a Roman Catholic historian, describes the province of Ulster as "the most constant in maintaining its liberty and in preserving the Catholic religion." The greater part of the bishops and ministers were still Roman Catholics, and of the few Protestant ministers, who were scattered over the country, many were shamefully ignorant, and even scandalous in their lives. In many parishes there was no minister, and except in some of the principal towns and cities, divine service had not been performed in a single parish church throughout the province for years together.

To provide a remedy for this unhappy state of the country, King James projected a plan for planting it with settlers from England and Scotland. Great part of the province had been forfeited to the crown during the rebellions, and from the forfeited estates liberal distribution was made for the encouragement of settlers; the King taking especial care, at the same time, to provide for the spread of religion, by repairing the churches and providing glebes for the ministers, as well as restoring the ecclesiastical possessions and endowing free schools for the revival of learning.

Soon after this plan was set on foot the province began to assume a new aspect. The deserted cities were filled with inhabitants, towns were built and incorporated, the lands gradually cleared of woods, cultivation was resumed, and peace and industry were generally restored. The sees were now all filled with Protestant Bishops, and a scriptural confession of faith, in which the intolerant spirit of the church of England was avoided, was drawn up by Dr. (afterwards Archbishop) Ussher, and adopted by the clergy; so that in the bosom of the church of Ireland many of the Puritans of England and Scotland, who had been driven, by persecution, from their native country, found a secure retreat, and were promoted to situations of honour and usefulness. Among the most eminent of these were Mr. Edward Brice, formerly minister of Stirling, who was settled at Broadisland in the year 1613; Mr. Hubbard, an English Puritan minister, settled at Carrickfergus about the year 1621; Mr. John Ridge, a native of England, presented in 1619 to the vicarage of Antrim; Mr. Robert Blair, formerly one of the regents or teachers in the College of Glasgow, who came to Bangor in 1623; and Mr. James Hamilton, who was educated for the ministry in Scotland, and ordained at Ballywater about the year 1625.

Before the arrival of these godly ministers the character of the settlers was far from being such as to encourage them in their labours, and indeed they were very generally openly immoral and profane. " From Scotland," says Mr. Stewart, who was minister of Donaghadee in 1645,*—" from Scotland came many, and from England not a few; yet all of them generally the scum of both nations, who, from debt, or breaking and fleeing from justice, or seeking shelter, came hither, hoping to be without fear of man's justice, in a land where there was nothing or but little as yet, of the fear of God. And in a few years there flocked such a multitude of people from Scotland, that these northern counties of Down, Antrim, Londonderry &c., were in a good measure planted, which had been waste before. Yet most of the people were all void of godliness, who seemed rather to flee from God in this enterprise than to follow their own mercy. Yet God followed them when they fled from him. Albeit at first it must be remembered, that as they cared little for any church, so God seemed to care as

---

* For this and the subsequent extracts from a manuscript of Mr. Stewart, as well as for the preceding account of the state of Ireland, and much of what follows, we are indebted to the excellent History of the Presbyterian Church in Ireland, by Dr. Reid, of Carrickfergus.

little for them. For these strangers were no better entertained than with the relics of Popery, served up in a ceremonial service of God, under a sort of antichristian hierarchy, and committed to the care of a number of careless men, who were only zealous to call for their gain from their quarter; men who said "come ye, I will bring wine, let us drink, for to-morrow shall be as this day, and much more abundant." Thus on all hands atheism increased, and disregard of God, iniquity abounded with contention, fighting, murder, adultery, &c. as among people who, as they had nothing within them to over-awe them, so their ministers' example was worse than nothing, for, from the prophets of Israel profaneness went forth to the whole land.   And verily at this time the whole body of this people seemed ripe for the manifestation, in a great degree, either of God's judgments or mercy.   For their carriage made them to be abhorred at home in their native land, inso-much that going for Ireland was looked on as a miserable mark of a deplorable person.   Yea, it was turned into a proverb, and one of the worst expressions of disdain that could be invented was, to tell a man that "Ireland would be his hinder end!" The labours by which the English and Scottish ministers above named endeavoured to establish the gospel among this ungodly people, were most zealous and un-remitting.   Some idea of them may be formed from the ac-count given by Mr. Blair of his own labours in the parish of Bangor.   "My charge," says he, "was very great, consist-ing of about six miles in length, and containing above 1200 persons come to age, besides children, who stood greatly in need of instruction.   This being the case, I preached twice every week, besides the Lord's day.   But finding still that this fell short of reaching the design of a gospel ministry, and that the most part continued vastly ignorant, I saw the necessity of trying a more plain and familiar way of instructing them; and therefore, besides my public preaching, I spent as much time every week, as my bodily strength could hold out with, in exhorting and catechising them.   Not long after I fell upon this method, the Lord visited me with a fever; on which, some who hated my painfulness in the ministry, said scoffingly, that they knew I could not hold out as I began.   But in a little space it pleased the Lord to raise me up again, and he enabled me to continue that method the whole time I was at Bangor."

To these labours, Mr. Blair and his brethren joined much fervent prayer.   Mr. Blair's acquaintance, with Mr. Cunning-ham of Holywood was comfortable to them both, and they frequently visited one another, and spent many days and hours together in prayer and godly conference.

The effects were soon apparent.   A spirit of religious in-quiry was excited among the people, ignorance began to be dispelled, careless and secure persons were aroused to a sense of their danger, the immoral were reclaimed to habits of decency, and the general aspect of the country became marvellously changed. At Bangor a considerable reformation was effected, and, a short time afterwards, a more general awakening appeared in the neighbourhood of Oldstone, where James Glendinning, a native of Scotland, and formerly Lecturer at Carrickfergus, had lately settled as minister.

Of the origin and progress of this awakening Mr. Stewart has preserved the following Account. " Mr. Blair," says he, " coming over from Bangor to Carrickfergus on some business, and occasionally hearing Mr. Glendinning preach, perceived some sparkles of good inclination in him, yet found him not solid but weak, and not fitted for a public place, and among the English. On which Mr. Blair did call him, and using freedom with him, advised him to go to some place in the country among his countrymen; whereupon he went to Oldstone (near the town of Antrim) and was there placed. He was a man who would never have been chosen by a wise assembly of ministers, nor sent to begin a reformation in this land. For he was little better than distracted; yea, afterwards, did actually become so. Yet this was the Lord's choice, to begin with him the admirable work of God; which I mention on purpose that all men may see how the glory is only the Lord's in making a holy nation in this profane land and that it was 'not by might nor by power, nor by man's wisdom, but by my Spirit, saith the Lord.' At Oldstone, God made use of him to awaken the consciences of a lewd and secure people thereabouts. For seeing the great lewdness and ungodly sinfulness of the people, he preached to them nothing but lawwrath, and the terrors of God for sin. And in very deed for this only was he fitted, for hardly could he preach any other thing. But behold the success! For the hearers finding themselves condemned by the mouth of God speaking in his word, fell into such anxiety and terror of conscience that they looked on themselves as altogether lost and damned; and this work appeared not in one single person or two, but multitudes were brought to understand their way, and to cry out, men and brethren, what shall we do to be saved! I have seen them myself stricken into a swoon with the word; yea, a dozen in one day carried out of doors as dead, so marvellous was the power of God smiting their hearts for sin, condemning and killing. And of these were none of the weaker sex or spirit, but indeed some of the boldest spirits who formerly feared not with their swords to put a whole market town in a fray; yet in defence of their stubbornness cared not to lie in prison and in the stocks; and being incorrigible, were as ready to do the like the next day. I have heard one of them, then a mighty strong man, now a mighty Christian, say that his end in coming to church was to consult with his companions how

to work some mischief. And yet at one of those sermons he
was so catched, that he was fully subdued. But why do I
speak of him? We knew and yet know, multitudes of such
men who sinned and still gloried in it because they feared no
man, yet are now patterns of sobriety, fearing to sin because
they fear God. And this spread through the country to admir
ation, especially to that river, commonly called the Six-mile-
water, for there this work began at first. At this time of
people's gathering to Christ, it pleased the Lord to visit mer-
cifully the honourable family in Antrim, so as Sir John
Clotworthy, and my lady his mother, and his own precious
lady, did shine in an eminent manner in receiving the gospel,
and offering themselves to the Lord; whose example instantly
other gentlemen followed, such as Captain Norton, of whom
the gospel made a clear and cleanly conquest.

"When, therefore, the multitude of wounded consciences
were healed, they began to draw into holy communion and
meeting together privately for edification, a thing which in a
lifeless generation is both neglected and reproved. But the
new life forced it among the people, who desired to know
what God was doing with the souls of their neighbours, who,
they perceived, were wrought on in spirit, as they had been.
There was a man in the parish of Oldstone, called Hugh
Campbell, who had fled from Scotland; him God caught in
Ireland, and made him an eminent and exemplary Christian
until this day. He was a gentleman of the house of Duket-
hall. After this man was healed of the wound given to his
soul by the Almighty he became very refreshful to others who
had less learning and judgment than himself. He therefore
invited some of his honest neighbours who fought the same
fight of faith, to meet him at his house on the last Friday of
the month; where and when, beginning with a few, they spent
their time in prayer, mutual edification, and conference on
what they found within them, nothing like the superficial
superfluous meetings of some cold-hearted professors, who
afterwards made this work a snare to many. But these new
beginners were more filled with heart exercise than head notions, and with fervent prayer rather than conceity gifts to
fill the head. As these truly increased so did this meeting
for private edification increase too; and still at Hugh
Campbell's house, on the last Friday of the month. At last
they grew so numerous, that the ministers who had begotten
them again to Christ, thought fit that some of them should
be still with them to prevent what hurt might follow."
Accordingly, adds Mr. Blair, "Mr. John Ridge the judicious
and gracious minister of Antrim, perceiving many people on
both sides of the Six-mile-water awakened out of their security,
made an overture that a monthly meeting might be set up at
Antrim, which was within a mile of Oldstone, and lay centrical

for the awakened persons to resort to, and he invited Mr Cunningham, Mr. Hamilton, and myself, to take part in that work, who were all glad of the motion, and heartily embraced it. This meeting was continued for many years. In the summer days four did preach; and when the day grew shorter, only three: And through the Lord's blessing on our labours, religion was spread throughout that whole county, and into the borders of some others. Mr. Glendinning was at the first glad of the confluence of people, but we not having invited him to bear a part in the monthly meeting he became so emulous, that, to preserve popular applause, he watched and fasted wonderfully. Afterwards he was smitten with a number of erroneous and enthusiastic opinions, and at last he set out on a visit to the seven churches of Asia."

Having lost this instrument, others more worthy were afterwards through the good providence of God, added to the ministry. "From Scotland," says Mr. Blair, "came over Mr. Josiah Welsh, son of the famous Mr. John Welsh, who both in Scotland and France was instrumental in converting and confirming many. A great measure of that spirit which wrought in and by the father, rested also upon the son. The last time I had been in Scotland, I met with him, and finding of how zealous a spirit he was, I exhorted him to hasten over to Ireland, where he would find work enough, and I hoped success too. And so it came to pass: For Mr. Welsh having been settled at Temple-Patrick, became a great blessing to that people. Next Mr. Henry Colvert, an Englishman, helper to Mr. Edward Bryce at Broadisland, was settled at Oldstone. This able minister having been of a fervent spirit, and vehement delivery in preaching, and withal very diligent, he was a blessing to that people. And after these two the Lord brought over to Lochlarne old Mr. George Dunbar, after he had been deposed from his ministry at Ayr by the High Commission, and banished by the Privy Council. At Larne the Lord did greatly bless his ministry, and he and the other two having joined the monthly meeting, the word of God grew mightily, and his gracious work prospered in our hands."

About the year 1630; Mr. John Livingston, assistant at Torphichen, having been oppressed by the bishops, went over to Ireland, where he was ordained at Killinchie. "Being a man of a gracious melting spirit he did much good, and the Lord was pleased greatly to bless his ministry." Much about the same time Mr. Andrew Stuart, "a learned gentleman and fervent in spirit," was settled at Dunagor, where his ministry was successful during the short time he lived.

The blessed work of conversion, which was of several years' continuance, had now spread beyond the bounds of Antrim and Down to the skirts of neighbouring counties; and the resort of people to the monthly meeting and communion occasions, and the appetite of the people, were become so great, that the ministers were sometimes constrained in sympathy to the people to venture beyond any preparation they had made for the season. " And indeed preaching and praying were so pleasant in those days, and hearers so eager and greedy, that no day was long enough nor no room great enough to answer their strong desires and large expectations."

The following very interesting particulars are given by Mr. Livingston, in his Memoirs. Referring to his settlement at Killinchie, he says, " Although the people were very tractable, yet they were generally very ignorant, and I saw no appearance of doing any good among them ; yet it pleased the Lord that in a short time some of them began to understand somewhat of their condition. Not only had we public worship free of any inventions of man, but we had also a tolerable discipline ; for after I had been some while among them, by the advice of heads of families, some ablest for that charge were chosen elders to oversee the manners of the rest, and some deacons to gather and distribute the collections. We met every week, and such as fell into notorious public scandals, we desired to come before us. Such as came were dealt with both in public and private to confess their scandal, in presence of the congregation, at the Saturday's sermon, before the communion, which was celebrated twice in the year,—such as would not come before us, or coming would not be convinced to acknowledge their fault before the congregation, upon the Saturday preceding the communion, their names, scandals, and impenitency were read out before the congregation, and they debarred from the communion, which proved such a terror that we found very few of that sort. We needed not to have the communion oftener, for there were nine or ten parishes within the bounds of twenty miles, or little more, wherein there were godly and able ministers, that kept a society together, and every one of these had the communion twice a-year, at different times, and had two or three of the neighbouring ministers to help thereat ; and most part of the religious people used to resort to the communions of the rest of the parishes. Most of all these ministers used ordinarily to meet the first Friday of every month at Antrim, where was a great and good congregation, and that day was spent in fasting and prayer, and public preaching. Commonly two preached every forenoon and two in the afternoon. We used to come together the Thursday night before and staid the Friday night after, and consulted about such things as concerned the carrying on of the work of God ; and these meetings amongst ourselves were sometimes as profitable as either presbyteries or synods. And out of these parishes now mentioned, and some others also, such as laid religion to heart, used to convene to these meetings, especially out of the Six-mile-water, which was nearest hand, and where was the greatest number of religious people. And frequently the Sabbath after the Friday's meeting, the communion was celebrated in one or other of these parishes. Among all these ministers, there was never any jar or jealousy, yea nor amongst the professors, the greatest part of them being Scots, and some good number of very gracious English; all whose contention was to prefer others to themselves. And although the gifts of the ministers were much different, yet it was no observed that the people followed any to the undervaluing or others. Many of these religious professors had been both ignorant and profane, and for debt and want and worse causes, had left Scotland, yet the Lord was pleased by his word to work such a change, I do not think there were more lively and experienced Christians any where, than were these at that time in Ireland, and that in good numbers, and several of them, persons of good outward condition in the world; but being lately brought in, the lively edge was not yet gone off them, and the perpetual fear that the bishops would put away their ministers, made them with great hunger wait on the ordinances. I have known them come several miles from their own houses, to communions, to the Saturday's sermon, and spend the whole Saturday night in several companies, sometimes a minister being with them, sometimes themselves alone, in conference and prayer, and then they have waited on the public ordinances the whole Sabbath, and spent the Sabbath night likewise, and yet at the Monday's sermon they were not troubled with sleepiness, and so have not slept till they went home. Because of their holy and righteous carriage, they were generally reverenced even by the graceless multitude among whom they lived. Some of them had attained such dexterity at expressing religious purposes, by the resemblance of worldly things, that being at feasts and meals in common inns, where were some ignorant and profane persons, they would among themselves entertain a spiritual discourse for a long time, and the others professed that although they spoke good English, they could not understand what they said. In those days it was no great difficulty for a minister to preach or pray in public or private, such was the hunger of the hearers, and it was hard to judge whether there was more of the Lord's presence in the public or private meetings."

The system of discipline referred to by Mr. Livingston, was the same as that observed in Mr. Blair's congregation, of the beneficial influence of which, in connexion with the faithful preaching of the word, Mr. Blair narrates the following instance. " A cunning adulterer who had continued long in that sin before I went to Bangor, and by bribing the bishop's official had concealed his wickedness, having been present at a sermon which I had on the parable of the Sower, it pleased the Lord so to reach his conscience, that he made confession of his great sin with many tears, and sought to be admitted to the public profession of his repentance. This the session readily agreed to, and he appeared publicly for several days, under very deep conviction, to the great affecting of the congregation, and lived ever after a reformed man so far as could be perceived."

There were now many converts in all the congregations which have been mentioned, and Satan observing the prosperity of the gospel amongst them set himself to perplex them by discrediting the work of God in their hearts. This he did by a counterfeit of the operation of the Holy Spirit on several persons at Lochlarne, whom he caused to cry out during public worship, and some of them were affected with convulsive pangs. The number of persons thus affected increased daily, and at first the ministers and people pitied them, hoping that the Holy Spirit was at work with them. But when they had conversed with them, and found that they did not discover any sense of their sinful state or any longing after a Saviour, the minister of the place wrote to his brethren, inviting them to come and examine the matter, who when they had spoken with them saw that it was a mere delusion of the destroyer. The next Sabbath, an ignorant person in Mr. Blair's congregation made a noise, but immediately, says Mr. B., "I was assisted to rebuke that lying spirit which disturbed the worship of God, and I charged the same in the name and authority of Jesus Christ, not to molest that congregation; and through God's mercy we met with no more of that sort."

Having thus been foiled in this attempt Satan now made a handle of his own device to stir up enemies against the faithful ministers. Archbishop Ussher's Confession of Faith had by this time been laid aside, and the ritual and ceremonies of the English Church having been adopted in its stead, the former moderation of the bishops was no longer continued. The ministers who had been most successful in promoting the work of reformation were accused to them of teaching that bodily convulsions were necessary to the new birth, and the bishop of the diocese at first suspended four of them from their labours; and then, after a short relaxation, obtained for them by Archbishop Ussher, he deposed all the four from their sacred office. The conduct of the people on this occasion strikingly illustrates the spirit of prayer which abounded among them. Mr. Blair having set out to London, with the view of obtaining a trial for himself and his brethren, "left many holy persons, wrestling with God for a comfortable issue. And indeed," says he, "they were a praying people for whom I undertook this journey. At my house two nights were spent every week in prayer; and though those who did bear chief burden therein were not above the rank of husbandmen yet they abounded in the grace and spirit of prayer. Other places were not short of, but rather excelled in that duty, and even in congregations who yet enjoyed their own pastors, many prayers were put up on our account, as I learned at my return."

When Mr. Blair returned, with a favourable answer from the King, the trial was still delayed, but the ministers continued to meet and pray with their people, until at the end of a twelvemonth they obtained a licence to preach publicly for six months. So great was Mr. Blair's astonishment at the news of this unlooked-for liberty that he did not sleep for three nights afterwards. The first, he says, was wholly spent in admiring the goodness of God; the second in thanksgiving with his people, who solemnly prayed with him; and the third he spent in preparation for his stated lecture, which occurred on the succeeding day. When he resumed this lecture he found a large congregation, not only of his own flock, but of many from neighbouring congregations; who, on hearing the gospel again publicly preached, were melted down into tears of joy. The monthly meeting at Antrim was also resumed, to the inexpressible joy of the people, and public worship being now freely permitted, they made more progress in the ways of the Lord than ever before. This liberty was however of short continuance. Mr. Blair and Mr. Dunbar, were soon deposed a second time from their office, and they concluded their ministry by celebrating the Lord's supper, and solemnly delivering up their flocks to the great Bishop of souls from whom they had received their sacred office. Five of the other ministers were afterwards deposed, and the work of revival was for a time much impeded. The number of the godly was, however, very considerable, many of whom, along with some of their ministers, came over to Scotland to escape the violence of the persecution which followed.

This persecution proceeded from the adherents of Episcopacy, who, headed by the haughty and cruel Earl of Strafford, imposed such heavy fines, and inflicted so severe imprisonments upon the Presbyterians, for refusing to take the oaths prescribed to them by government, that while many of the ministers were forced to leave the country those who remained dared not preach publicly. They still however continued to meet privately with their people, and usually in the night time, for religious worship. And even when most of the ministers had fled to Scotland, and the more timid of those who still remained were afraid to attend these proscribed assemblies, such laymen as were most distinguished for their knowledge and piety conducted the worship of the people, and expounded the scriptures for their mutual edification and comfort. By these means the knowledge and love of the truth were preserved among multitudes, until they again had an opportunity of statedly hearing the gospel from the lips of their ministers, while others held the ministers in so great veneration that many of them removed to Scotland for the sole purpose of enjoying their ministry, and of those who remained large numbers came over from Ireland to attend the stated dispensation of the Lord's supper in the parishes where they were settled. On one occasion no fewer than 500 persons visited Stranraer, that they might receive ordinances from the hands of Mr. Livingston.

This first persecution was soon followed by a second of a more bloody and disastrous character, at the Rebellion of 1641—of which all classes of Protestants were the subjects, so violent, that in a small part of Ulster alone about thirty ministers were cruelly massacred by the papists.

These disasters put a check for the present to the progress of the Revival. In Scotland the ministers and people who had fled thither for refuge, were kindly treated by the people of God, and hid as it were in the hollow of His hand, until the times of slaughter and persecution had in some measure passed away. After a few years most of them returned to their adopted land; and along with the chaplains of the Scottish army, and many of the ministers, who had formerly adhered to Episcopacy, were the means of planting in Ulster the Presbyterian Church, which to the present day continues to flourish in that province.

Among the means by which this extensive work of grace was promoted, the christian character of the ministers, and their faithful and diligent preaching, hold a prominent place. The following particulars of their style of preaching may be added to what has already been said.—Of Mr. Brice, Mr. Livingston informs us, " that in all his preaching he insisted most on the life of Christ in the heart, and the light of his word and Spirit on the mind, which was his own continual exercise." "Mr. Ridge," he says "used not to have many points in his sermon, but he so enlarged those he had, that it was scarcely possible for any hearer to forget his preaching. He was a great urger of charitable works, and a very humble man." Mr. Blair's labours have already been particularly referred to. " He was a man," says Livingston, "of notable constitution both of body and mind; of a majestic, awful, yet affable and amiable countenance and carriage, thoroughly learned, or strong parts, deep invention and judgment, and of a most public spirit for God. His gift of preaching was such, that seldom could any observe withdrawing of assistance in public, which in others is frequent. He seldom ever wanted assurance of his salvation. He spent many days and nights in prayer alone and with others, and was vouchsafed great

intimacy with God." Of Mr. Welsh, we are informed by the
same writer, that " he was much exercised in his own spirit,
and therefore much of his preaching was an exercise of conscience ;" and Mr. Blair adds, " He did with great eagerness
convince the secure, and sweetly comfort those who were
dejected." " Mr. Stuart," says Livingston, " was a man
very straight in the cause of God." Of Mr. Colvert, he says,
" He very pertinently cited much scripture in his sermons,
and frequently urged private fasting and prayer." Mr. Livingston himself was the minister who was honoured when a
young man to preach the famous sermon at the Kirk of Shotts,
which was followed with so rich a blessing. He was one
of the most learned and laborious among the brethren.

Connected with the preaching of the gospel, it appears from
the foregoing narrative, that the strict and impartial exercise
of discipline—the frequent practice of public and private
fasting—the fellowship and godly conferences of Christians—
and above all, a spirit of earnest prayer, hold a prominent
place among the means of promoting this revival.

These means were all of the most scriptural kind, and without them it would be presumptuous to expect an extensive
revival of religion. Let then those amongst us who desire to
obtain a similar out-pouring of the Spirit of grace imitate the
example of these followers of Christ—let the gospel be
preached, with application to the consciences of men as sinners, and let it be adorned by the lives of those who profess
to receive it—let the discipline of the Church be impartially
and vigorously administered—the practice of fasting and social
prayer revived, and a spirit of enlarged intercession and supplication cherished—and then indeed may we hope to see
the windows of heaven opened, and a blessing poured out
" till there shall not be room enough to hold it." Surely this
is a blessing worthy of being asked, and if sought for the result is not doubtful. The Saviour himself has assured us
that if we " being evil know how to give good gifts to our
children, *much more* will our heavenly Father give HIS HOLY
SPIRIT to them that ask Him." " Ask, and ye shall receive,
seek, and ye shall find ; knock, and it shall be opened unto
you, for I say unto you that *every one* that asketh receiveth,
and he that seeketh findeth, and to him that knocketh it
shall be opened." " For as the earth bringeth forth her bud,
and as the garden causeth the things that are sown in it to
spring forth, so the Lord God will cause righteousness and
praise to spring forth before all the nations."

REVIVALS OF RELIGION.

No. VIII.

ISLAND OF LEWIS, 1824—1835.

Extracted from a work recently published by Oliphant and Son, "History of Revivals of Religion in the British Isles, especially in Scotland"—a volume which ought to be perused by every Christian.

THE following narrative relates chiefly to the parish of Uig, and gives a most interesting sketch of a work of divine grace which has been in progress there for the last eleven years, and which is still going on: and it plainly demonstrates that the gospel is "the power of God" in renewing the soul of fallen man, for to no other means can the happy results which have taken place there be ascribed.

Very soon after the settlement of the present minister of Uig, an awakening took place amongst the people who had previously been mere formalists. Presently inquirers came to obtain private instruction, and the exigencies of the people led to the extension of religious opportunities—such as a lecture on Thursdays, and many regular prayer meetings, which still exist, and are attended with avidity. When Mr. M'Leod first entered on his office, all the people of a certain age were accustomed to flock to the table of communion, but as he had reason to apprehend that few of them discerned the Lord in the feast, he preached to them carefully for a year, before he ventured to celebrate that solemn ordinance. And so much had their light increased, that only a small portion of the old communicants presented themselves, and they with silent tears. It is very remarkable, that in the course of years wherein he acted as their pastor, he has scarcely been obliged to reject or keep back any one from this feast of love. Indeed there are many whom their pastor would be glad to admit, who keep back, perhaps from some erroneous apprehension of the nature of the ordinance. This is the case in several other Highland parishes. At the communion services of 1828, the island seemed to be moved with one emotion, for 9000 people flocked to Uig on that occasion. Then and subsequently, the days and nights, from the fast to the thanksgiving days, have been occupied in exhortation and prayer, by the various ministers and elders, amongst whom the name of John Macdonald of Farintosh or Urquhart, stands pre-eminent. In 1834, an immense concourse of persons attended, following and seeking the truth, from the Isles of Harris and Uist, as they had done for a year or two before ; and the cautious pastor, speaking of this and similar occasions, describes to a Christian friend the "deep impression" which was then made, the "deepening work," the " new and old converts," the "liberty of the ministers in preaching," the " refreshment of the people in hearing," and the " fervent longing for another such season." He also speaks of " the knowledge and experience of the people," of the " Gospel prospering in Lewis," and of "many new converts being brought in during the solemnities."

It is not in our power to give much particular detail, the honourable and judicious caution of the faithful pastor, for the present declining to bring into public view the cases of individuals in whose real devotion to God he has much comfort. General results, however, are in the possession of the public, and may be thankfully and humbly stated, to the praise of that blessed Spirit who has wrought such changes.

In proof of the minister's own enjoyment of his scene of labour it is pleasing to state, that he remarks in 1834 : "Ten winters have I passed here, all wonderfully short, pleasant, and delightful ;" and his teachers are all so much interested in their occupation, that they would rather expend their lives in that retired region than remove to wealthier and more southern districts. We hope the faithful records preserved by him who watches for their souls, as one who must give account, will, at no distant day, be published to revive the drooping Church. In the mean time, all that we are about to relate of the general aspect of society there, we mention as detailed by witnesses much interested in stating the truth correctly.

1. *The prayerfulness of the people.*—One gentleman, who annually visits the Lewis, mentions that he has often walked forth at eventide, to have his spirit refreshed by observing the devotional temper of the people of Uig— and that, at all hours, from eight o'clock at night till one in the morning, he has passed by and overheard persons

engaged in prayer. Many a bush formed a shelter for a soul communing with its God; and along the brown ridges of the fallow, by stooping, so as to cast the figures between the eye and the clear margin of the horizon, dim forms might be discerned, either alone, or two and three together, kneeling and pouring out their wants at the footstool of mercy. The captain of a king's ship, which lay for a considerable time off the island, who, in pursuing his sports, had crossed and recrossed the lands in all directions, bears witness that he never met any intoxication—any profanity, nor indeed a single person engaged in any occupation which might tempt him to wish to shrink from public inspection, except during their frequent retirements for prayer. He mentioned, in particular, his having entered a woodyard in the town of Stornoway, to enquire into the progress of some repairs making on his boat, when he saw two men retire behind the logs to pray together; and, though their Gælic was unintelligible to him, their occupation, and obvious abstraction from the world, and solemn impression of the divine presence, softened and subdued the man of the sea, though not given to the melting mood. He said, " they are extraordinary people here; one cannot but be struck with their honesty, kindness, and sobriety. I am told they make a good deal of whisky for sale. It cannot be for home consumption, for I think I never met a drunk person out of the town. One hears of religion elsewhere, but one sees it here in every thing."

We have pleasure in mentioning, as another example of the devotional habits of these people, what a friend who was rowed up the Loch Roag witnessed. The way being long, it is customary to stop to rest and refresh the oarsmen. When they had drawn their boat up into the little bay, and ceased from their toil, the men, before they tasted of their food, raised their blue bonnets, and united in prayer.

It may be proper to state, that the cabins of the inhabitants, consisting of but one apartment, furnish no opportunity of retirement; and this explains, in part, the custom of praying in the open air. There is, however, another and more affecting reason. The people want to repair far more frequently to the footstool of mercy than at morning and evening; and as their occupations are in general out of doors, or on the waves, so also are their prayers.

There are five natives of the parish of Uig who were enlisted when a regiment was raised on the island, and having gone with the army to Egypt, lost their sight by ophthalmy, and after their return have become acquainted with the doctrines of the gospel. It is common with them to bless God for having taken away their bodily eyes, since they regard that as one of the instruments in his hand for opening the mental sight, which was before in a state of darkness. Three of them are active fellow-helpers in the extension of Christian truth and consolation. One is a most efficient and zealous elder in the parish of Uig; of another we shall have occasion to relate a curious circumstance under the head of liberality.

2. *The uprightness of the people.*—On occasion of a year of famine, the natives were put to great straits, and in danger of perishing for want. A vessel, laden with meal was driven upon their shores by stress of weather. Did the famine-stricken natives seize on the ship, and lawlessly apply her cargo to the supply of their necessities? If they had, hunger would have formed for them a plausible excuse. Twenty years before they would doubtless have done so, and held themselves guiltless. But now it was not so. Every portion was accurately weighed or divided; and, as their necessities were so great that they had nothing then to pay, their affectionate minister gave a promissory note for it, knowing well that the excellent lady whose property the lands are, would not suffer him to be impoverished. The people knew this also, but none took advantage of it, all were occupied in economising to the utmost, till one after another they had repaid their debt. Thus they obtained not only the great blessing of necessary food, but preserved the still greater blessing of integrity, and a spirit free from covetousness.

It is a rule in this and the other isles of the Hebrides, that when a man meets a stray sheep on the moor, he is entitled to carry it home as his own, and obliged to make an equivalent offering in the collection for the poor on the Sabbath day. After the commencement of the revival in the Lewis, many came to confess to their minister the trouble of conscience they experienced by reason of having what they called a black sheep in their flocks—some having had them for several winters. The minister always directed them to make restitution now in the appointed way; and in one season, the sum of £16 was deposited in the plate. The number of sheep annually lost has wonderfully diminished since the commencement of the revival, leading to the conclusion, that the loss imputed to accident arose from dishonesty.

3. *The Christian liberality of the people.*—It has long been the custom to make a collection at the Thursday lecture, for the most necessitous persons in the district where the lecture is held—and thus, without poor rates, these people support their own poor. For many years they have contributed £13 or upwards to the Gælic School Society, sometimes £16, and one year, when the Society was in difficulty, the contribution amounted to £20. On transmitting £16, which was the sum collected in Uig in 1830, Mr. M'Leod remarks—" Considering the circumstances of the people, I bear testimony, that their liberality and zeal in this case have cause to provoke very many to similar duties. It was most delightful to see the hoary head, and the young scholar of eight or nine years, joining in this contribution. The will preponderates over our purse, so that we cannot do exactly what we would." In 1831, Mr. M'Leod, while he petitions that a teacher may not be removed from his present station for another year, says, " a poor man in that station declared to me lately, that should the directors demand one of his cows, he would readily give one before he would part with the teacher."

The journal of the superintendent, in stating the examination of one of the schools in Uig, mentions the case of a man, named Norman M'Leod, who is one of the many hundreds of souls on the isle of Lewis, that have come out of gross darkness, into the sweet and blessed light of the knowledge of God, partly by means of the Gælic schools, and partly by the ministration of the truth. " Norman M'Leod is a native of this parish, and at an early age enlisted into the army, went abroad, and was in several engagements." "Balls," says he, " whizzing about me in numbers, but the Lord directed them so that they did me no harm." He was in Egypt, and there lived in drunkenness and profligacy. " There," says he in his native Gælic, " the Lord took from me my bodily sight. I came home, and on the way was wonderfully preserved. At length I found myself in my native land. Here I found things not as I left them. I found the Bible of God, of which I was totally ignorant, among my friends; and schools amongst them for teaching the knowledge of that blessed book. I found such a work among them with Bibles and schools as was altogether new to me. Nay the very children would correct and reprove me, though an old man. In one of these schools the Bible caught my ear; it sunk into my heart; it there opened an eye that sin had ever kept sealed; it read to me my deeds; it led me to trace my former ways; yea, times, places, and deeds that were quite banished from my memory, were recalled into full view. It recorded a black catalogue against me, ard seemed to fix my portion amongst the damned. I thought my case altogether a hopeless one, but the same Bible brought to my ears tidings of unutterable worth—salvation through a crucified Saviour."

The superintendent mentions this as a preface to a little story, "which, were the honesty and simplicity of the old man known to the reader, would be considered more interesting still."

" I began," said Norman to his minister, " to think how these Gælic schools came to be planted in my country. I thought on the state of my country when I knew it before in my youth, and on the blessed fruits of these schools among my kindred. I contrasted both, and wondered, and thought, and wondered again. Said I, what is this? What a change of things! Blessed God! Blessed Bible! Blessed people, that sent these schools! and blessed schools, that teach the Bible of God to perishing sinners! and blessed teachers, men of Christ! I thought what would my poor country be, but for the Bible and these schools. I was led into their history, and traced them to a Society in Edinburgh. They engrossed my attention, and I thought them really the schools of Christ. I thought I would pray for them, and so I did; but this, thought I, is not enough. When the Lord took away my eyesight, he gave me a pension; I thought I should give some of that to help his schools. A public collection was proposed by you. I felt happy at this, and prayed that the Lord might open na sporain dhubhà (that is, the black purses, an appellation given to the purses of greedy worldlings), and I myself gave two shillings. When a collection was proposed this year, ' I think,' said I to myself, ' I shall give this year four shillings—double what I gave last.' ' It is enough for you,' said something within me, ' to give what you gave last year—two shillings.' " Here follows a long and most original debate, between Norman with the enlarged and melted heart, and the old worldly-wise Norman. Sometimes he would give double, then five, then ten, then back to five. During all this debate he was in great agitation, having, as he felt, lifted up his hand to the Lord that he would give so much. He thought of Ananias and Sapphira, and dared not go back; while the same inward voice asked him, "'Ah! Norman, what are you about, you are now going crazy altogether; you are a poor blind man, you cannot work, you have a family of seven to support, and the money God gave you as a provision for your family, you should apply to the object for which it was given, which will be most acceptable to Him,' &c.

" I then began to ruminate on the whole process, and at length I thought my opposition might be the suggestion of Satan, to keep me from giving so much to the cause of Christ. On reflecting on this for a while, I felt convinced it was he. I started upon my legs, and, lifting up my hand with defiance, I said, 'Ah! you devil, I will give a score of them. I will give a pound note every year I live, so the farther you follow me, the more you shall lose.' From that moment the temptation ceased."

In 1835, when in addition to all their usual collections, they in one day at church gathered £20 for church extension, they were favoured with such a successful fishing season, as enabled them to supply all the wants of the winter. The fishing had for many years failed; and the people observed that, by means of this wealth bestowed on them from the sea in 1835, they were amply repaid for all they had been enabled to give. This is another of those facts which we note to the glory of Him who is nigh unto all them that fear him. He knoweth what we have need of, and they who scatter in faith shall still increase. Let not any of those contributors shrink from this mention of the gracious dealing of God with them. The effort of their liberality was known to those interested in the Church Extension Scheme, and the plentiful fishing was told in the newspapers. May those who see the divine hand give Him the praise!

One feature of this revival peculiarly interesting, is that souls of all ages have been affected, from the infant of three years to the man verging on a hundred. We present a notice of the youngest, and one of the oldest within our knowledge.

Catherine Smith was a native of Pabay, a small island in Loch Roag, where dwell seven families. From their insular situation and poverty, it has not been in the power of the parents to educate their children; but little Kitty is an example of the truth, that all God's children are taught of him; for, when only two years old, she was observed to lay aside her playthings, and clasp her little hands with reverence during family worship; and at th age of three she was in the habit of repeating the 23rd Psalm, with such relish and fervour, as showed that she looked to the good Shepherd in the character of a lamb of his flock. Her parents taught her also the Lord's Prayer, which she repeated duly, not only at her stated times, but often in the silence of the night. She frequently pressed the duty of prayer, not only on the other children, but on her parents; and she told her father that, in their absence, when she would ask a blessing on the food left for the children, her brothers and sisters would mock at and beat her for doing so.

The Rev. J. Macdonald of Farintosh having preached in the parish of Uig, Kitty's parents were among the many who went to hear him. On their return they mentioned what he had said about the formality of much that is called prayer, and the ignorance of many as to its spirituality; they stated, according to their recollection of the sermon, that many had old useless prayers, and greatly needed to learn to pray with the Spirit. The child observed this, and two days after, said to her mother, "it is time for me to give over my old form of prayer." Her mother replied, "neither you nor your prayers are old;" but she rejoined, I must give them over, and use the prayers which the Lord will teach me." After this she withdrew to retired spots for prayer. At one time her younger sister returned without her, and on being asked where she had left Kitty, she said, "I left her praying." Her father says that he has often sat up in the bed listening to her sweet young voice, presenting this petition with heartfelt earnestness, "Oh, redeem me from spiritual and eternal death."

From the remoteness of her dwelling, Kitty had never attended any place of public worship,—but the Sabbath was her delight,—and often would she call her brothers and sisters from the play in which they were thoughtlessly engaged, asking them to join in prayer and other devout exercises, and warning them, that if they profaned the day, and disliked God's worship, they must perish. Her mother observing the intent gaze with which she looked on a large fire, enquired what she saw in that fire? She replied, "I am seeing that my state would be awful if I were to fall into that fire, even though I should be immediately taken out; but woe is me, those who are cast into hell fire will never come out thence." Another day, when walking by the side of a precipice, and looking down, she exclaimed to her mother, " how fearful would our state be if we were to fall down this rock, even though we should be lifted up again; but they that are cast into the depths of hell will never be raised therefrom."

One day her mother found her lying on a bench with a sad countenance, and addressed some jocular words to her with a view to cheer her. But the child's heart was occupied with solemn thoughts of eternity; and instead of smiling she answered gravely, "Oh, mother, you are vexing my spirit, I would rather hear you praying." In truth, eternity was very near her, and the Spirit of God was preparing her for it. As she got up one morning, she said, " Oh, are we not wicked creatures who have put Christ to death?" Her mother, curious to hear what one so young could say on such a subject, replied, " Christ was put to death, Kitty, long before we were born." The child, speaking with an understanding heart, said, " Mother, I am younger than you, but my sins were crucifying him." After a pause, she added, " what a wonder that Christ could be put to death when he himself was God, and had power to kill every one, indeed they only put him to death as man, for it is impossible to kill God." She used often to repeat passages from Peter Grant's spiritual songs, such as, "It is the blood of the Lamb that precious is." When she came to the conclusion of the verse, "It is not valued according to its worth," she would, in touching terms, lament the sad truth, that His blood is so lightly thought of. Being present when some pious persons spoke of those in Rev. vii, who have washed their robes and made them white in the blood of the Lamb, she said, "Is it not wonderful that, while other blood stains what is dipt in it, this cleanses and makes white?"

Murdoch M'Leod being engaged in the valuable duties of a Scottish elder in the little island of Pabay, Kitty wished to hear him, but from bashfulness was ashamed to enter the house where he was employed in worship; she therefore climbed up to the window and sat there till all was over. Being asked what she had heard, she said she was amazed to hear that Christ offered himself as a Saviour to many in our land who rejected him, and that he was now going to other and more remote quarters to win souls. She then added with the pathos of a full heart, " Oh, who knows but he may return here again !"

Soon after she had completed her seventh year, sne was attacked by that sickness which opened her way to the kingdom of Heaven, and in December, 1829, this lowly child was carried from her poor native island to the blessed region where the redeemed of the Lord find their home; and her name has left a sweet perfume behid it.

From this most satisfactory and authentic account of the blessed state of one of the youngest souls brought to Christ, during the revival at the Lewis, which strongly reminds us of the narrative of a child of equally tender years detailed by Jonathan Edwards, we turn to an aged man named Malcolm M'Leod. Malcolm had reached the great age of 95, without experiencing repentance unto life. Infirmity had for some time prevented him from attending public worship, and as far as man might judge, his decaying faculties were fast shutting up the avenues to the soul, and he was less likely than many to become the subject of converting grace. But the Lord saw it not so. In October or November, 1834, his pious daughter brought home notes of a sermon she had been hearing, which were made the means of serious impression to her father, and he is going on in a very promising progress in the divine life. Though he is becoming blind with age, his mental faculties are entire, and the whole man is enlivened, having received a stimulus which arouses his attention, sharpens his understanding, and interests his heart. Instead of dozing away his hours, he now sleeps very little; prayer and praise have also become his principal food. His glad pastor says of him, " He is a most interesting sight, caught at the eleventh hour; O how wonderful are the ways of sovereign grace!" With his usual faithfulness, Mr. M'Leod ministers to him in private, and lately preached at his bedside, on the man who was thirtyeight years at the pool. And at the last season of communion the venerable man was borne by four friends and placed at the table of his Lord, with tears of sorrow for past profanation of that privilege, coursing each other over his furrowed cheeks, and of grateful love for present blessings. The whole multitude were moved, every eye glistening in sweet sympathy with his feelings. When we hear such things, may we not justly exclaim, "what has God wrought!"

In 1835, the Rev. A. M'Leod visited some of the other western isles to ascertain their state, and was much moved to see the isle of Tyree in particular, fortified against gospel truth, by the opposition of those having influence, and the natural ignorance and corruption of the people. His heart has not found rest without suggesting means to "assault the ancient garrison," so that they may in the Lord's good time subdue and "drive the Canaanite out of the land." But that which brings the visit to Tyree under our peculiar notice, is the effect produced on the people of Uig, when their pastor again reached home, and related to them what he had witnessed. He frequently had occasion to observe, that after a short absence, not only was the love of his people increased, but their zeal to run their Christian course also. On hearing of the deplorable ignorance and wickedness to be met with in the isle of Tyree, several of Mr. M'Leod's people who were then as careless as they, were brought under concern ; and when they heard of the religious views entertained by some of these islanders, they were convicted with having secretly cherished similar opinions, although they were daily favoured with gospel ordinances. Since November in particular, there has been much religious impression amongst the people, silent tears, in general, pervading the whole congregation. This used to be the case during the long time that worship was held in the field, while the church was building, but had subsided in a degree since they occupied the new church, till this fresh awakening has melted many new hearts, and refreshed many who had been previously awakened. It is a fact worthy of observation, that during ten years in which this work of grace has made a steady progress, there has not been one outbreaking of enthusiasm, or delusion, or false doctrine, so that their minister expressed great astonishment and thankfulness, after reading Dr. Sprague's work on American Revivals, that they have been so graciously preserved from the extravagance and error which has in some few instances broken in to injure the integrity of the work in America.

In considering the state of things in the parish of Uig, we are disposed to rejoice over it more than over any other

Scottish Revival. Its calm, and deep, and prolonged flow, and its sincerity, may be imputed to some natural and obvious causes. God has vouchsafed to them for ten years the ministrations of a man, whose method is consistent, and now well understood by them. He has been preserved in prayerful humility as their watchman, and saved from in any way casting a stumblingblock in their way. The ministers who have been placed in the neighbouring churches (two of which are government churches that have within a few years been opened on the island) are men who greatly strengthen his hands by preaching not "another gospel" but the same doctrine with himself, thus avoiding distraction and perplexity. Though Uig be the most enlivened spot, the revival is by no means limited to that parish. There has been no variety of sects introducing controversy and strife, or withdrawing men's minds from the essentials that concern their own souls, to fix them on the less weighty forms of church government, or questions of no profit. In this respect, truth has had a fairer entrance to the mind, and prayer has not been hindered. At Arran there seemed to be a tendency in some to yield to bodily excitement and nervous emotions, which their results proved not to have been genuine workings of the renewed heart. In Glenlyon, the spirit of controversy met and drove back the spirit of contrition. At Moulin, the removal of the faithful instructor left the sheep to be scattered. But in Lewis, hitherto the Lord hath upheld and sheltered his flock from such dangers, and the spirit of faith and prayer and a sound mind is preserved amongst them. May it never die away, but from this distant spot of our empire may the blessed wave of salvation swell and rise, till it shall overflow the land, and gather in every county, every parish, and every soul to the kingdom of our God and of his Christ!

REVIVALS OF RELIGION.

No. IX.

WALES, 1649—1794.

WHILE the efforts of the Reformers from Popery were exerted to spread abroad the blessed light of the Reformation throughout England and Scotland, the principality of Wales seems to have been comparatively neglected. This may have been owing to the difference of language and the difficulty of access to a population scattered over a mountainous country.

Shortly after the meeting of the famous Westminster Assembly, public attention was directed to the spiritual condition of Wales. It was found on inquiry that the inhabitants were in a most destitute state as regarded the means of religious instruction : the few clergymen they had were ignorant and idle, and the people had neither bibles nor catechisms in their own language. The Parliament, taking their case into consideration, on the 22nd February, 1649, passed an Act for the better propagation of the Gospel in Wales ; and, for carrying the Act into effect, appointed commissioners to visit the country, and ascertain the destitution, and apply an immediate remedy. Such was the diligence of the commissioners in this good work, that in the short space of three years they settled one hundred and fifty pious ministers in the thirteen Welsh counties ; and in every market town they had placed one schoolmaster, and in the larger towns two, all of them men who had received a university education. In the prosecution of their work, the commissioners found great difficulty in procuring a succession of ministers able to preach in the Welsh language. And in order to meet the exigency of the case, they appointed thirty preachers to itinerate over the country ; these, however, were found insufficient for overtaking the destitution, and to supply the deficiency, they permitted persons of approved piety to go amongst the people to read to them the Bible, and converse with them about those things that pertained to their everlasting peace.

These exertions on the part of the government ended with the restoration of Charles the Second ; and the further improvement of Wales was left very much to the individual exertions of persons specially raised up by Providence for the work. One of those instruments was Mr. Hugh Owen. He was a candidate for the ministry when the Act of Uniformity came forth, and not feeling himself at liberty to comply with its terms, he settled down in Merionethshire, upon an estate of his own in that county, and occupied his time in preaching the Gospel to the poor ignorant people: his manner was affectionate and moving, and many were much benefitted by his preaching. He went about declaring the Gospel of salvation throughout Merionethshire, and the neighbouring counties of Montgomery and Caernarvon. He had stations in all these places, some of them twenty and thirty miles from his own residence. He performed his circuit in about three months, and then began again. Great numbers attended his ministry. He laboured indefatigably, and impaired his health by riding often during the night, and in cold stormy weather, over the mountains. He was a primitive apostolical Christian, meek and humble; and would often style himself less than the least of all the ministers of Jesus Christ. He died, after a life of much usefulness, in 1697, aged 62. Another benefactor to Wales was Mr. Thomas Gouge. He was ejected from St. Sepulchre's, London, by the Act of Uniformity. Prevented by this odious enactment from exercising his ministry, Providence directed his attention to Wales; and at the advanced age of between 60 and 70 years, he began itinerating through that country, preaching the Gospel; and although much opposed he remembered the injunction of his Master, "when they persecute you in this city, flee ye into another." Not content with preaching to the old, he set about providing means of instruction for the young, and was instrumental in establishing free Schools in many of the towns he visited. He also got printed an edition of eight thousand copies of the Scriptures in the Welsh language; one thousand of which he gave gratis to those who were unable to pay, and the rest were sold at a reduced price. In addition to this, he got printed for the schools, a catechism and several other useful books, all in the native tongue. From an account, published in 1675, of his labours, we find that he had established schools in fifty-one of the chief towns in Wales, and that in these schools there were upwards of one thousand children under instruction. To support these schools, Mr. Gouge was much assisted with funds by the friends of religion in London and elsewhere. In this good work he employed all his time, and engaged in it with his whole heart; and though in his seventy-fifth year, he still, once a-year, and sometimes even oftener, travelled over the greater part of Wales. Such was his love and zeal for the salvation of souls, and diligence and activity in the prosecution of his work, that all the pains and difficulties he had to encounter seemed nothing, if he could only follow the example of his Master in going about doing good.

Nothing particular occurred in the way of exertion to promote religion in Wales, till the beginning of the last century, when it pleased God to raise up and qualify the Rev. Griffith Jones of Llandower, Carmarthenshire, who at this period showed himself a true friend to his countrymen, by the faithfulness of his preaching, and unbounded charity and benevolence. He was instrumental in procuring for Wales, two editions of the Bible, and in establishing Free Schools for the children of the poor in many parts of the principality. From the year 1737 to 1760, he published an annual account of their progress, and in the last mentioned year, their number had amounted to 215 Schools, attended by 8687 Scholars. Mr. Jones was an animated, faithful, and laborious minister, well versed in the Scriptures, and was honoured with much success. He did not confine his labours to his own flock, but frequently itinerated throughout the neighbouring parishes. It has been said that Mr. Howel Harris was one of the fruits of his ministry. This gentleman was a native of Trevecca, in Brecknockshire. He intended to enter the ministry in connection with the Established Church, and with this view entered himself a Student in one of the colleges at Oxford. He soon became disgusted at the conduct he witnessed there, and returned to his friends in Wales. He was not long at home before he ventured to go from house to house in his native parish, to speak to the people about their everlasting interests. He gradually extended his labours to the adjoining parishes: his fame soon spread over the whole country, and great multitudes attended his meetings. It is said that such was the power and authority with which he delivered his exhortations, that many could not refrain from crying out aloud, being overpowered by a sense of their own sinfulness in the sight of a holy God. Family worship was now set up in many a house which hitherto had never heard the voice of prayer. The enemy could no longer remain inactive, and offered every opposition in his power by means of mocking, derision, and threatening. Nothing daunted by these annoyances, Mr. Harris persevered in his labours of love. About the year 1736, he established a school at Trevecca, to which many of the youth came to be more largely instructed in the things which concerned their souls. The success which attended his labours among the young in Trevecca, encouraged Mr. Harris to establish in several other places, regular meetings of serious persons for prayer and religious conversation. This was the commencement of the private societies which have ever since formed a principal feature by which the Welsh Calvinistic Methodists may be distinguished from other denominations of professing Christians in that country. The number of these meetings rapidly increased; for in the short space of three years there were no less than 300 Societies in South Wales, all of them owing their origin to Mr. Harris's exertions. Referring to this period in a letter to the Rev. George Whitefield, Mr. Harris thus writes. "I have most glorious news to send you from Wales of the success attending brother Rowlands and many others. They are wounded by scores, and flock to hear the word by thousands. There is another clergyman coming out sweetly and united to us, and another young curate not far from Mr. Griffith Jones under strong drawings and convictions. There are now in Wales ten clergymen who are wonderfully owned of, by the Lord Jesus Christ—five beneficed and five settled in curacies." The first minister of the Establishment who ventured to assist Mr. Harris in promoting the spread of religion in Wales, was the Reverend and justly renowned Daniel Rowlands of Llangeitho. Such was this minister's popularity and eloquence, that persons have been known to come the distance of 100 miles to hear him preach, and attend the dispensation of the Lord's Supper. Under his ministry there were several awakenings to a considerable extent. The first took place when he was at prayer in the church; the effect was astonishing : the people were melted into tears and wept loudly. This awakening spread throughout the three parishes under his pastoral care, and many were savingly impressed. The next commenced at a prayer meeting in Llangeitho chapel. Six or seven of these Revivals took place during the life-time of Mr. Rowlands, some of them occurring at intervals of seven years. Speaking of this period, Whitefield remarks, in his own warm energetic language, "Blessed be God, there seems to be a noble spirit gone out into Wales. People make nothing of coming twenty miles to hear a sermon, and great numbers there are who have not only been hearers but doers also of the word, so that there is a most comfortable prospect of the spreading of the Gospel in Wales." At one of these awakenings it is said many hundreds, and even thousands were understood to be savingly impressed. One of the happy fruits of Mr. Rowland's ministry was the Rev. Thomas Charles, afterwards of Bala, a memoir of whom has been published by the Rev. Edward Morgan, and to which we are indebted for the narrative of the revival of religion at Bala under Mr. Charles's ministry. We shall give the narrative of Mr. Charles's reception of the truth in his own words :—

"On January 20, 1773, (in his eighteenth year,) I went to hear Mr. Rowland preach at Newchapel; his text was Heb. iv. 15. This is a day much to be remembered by me as long as I live. Ever since that happy day I have lived in a new heaven and a new earth. The change which a blind man who receives his sight experiences, does not exceed the change which at this time I experienced in my mind. It was then I was first convinced of the sin of unbelief, or of entertaining narrow, contracted, and hard thoughts of the Almighty. I had such a view of Christ as our High Priest, of his love, compassion, power, and all-sufficiency, as filled my soul with astonishment, with joy unspeakable, and full of glory ; my mind was overwhelmed and filled with amazement.

The truths exhibited to my view appeared for a time too wonderfully gracious to be believed; I could not believe for very joy; I had before some ideas of the Gospel work floating in my head, but they never powerfully and with divine energy penetrated my heart till now." Two years after this remarkable event in Mr. Charles's history, Providence very unexpectedly opened a way for his being educated for the ministry at Oxford, where he remained till 1778, when he was ordained to preach the everlasting Gospel. Few men have entered into the ministry more deeply impressed with the solemn responsibility attached to the right performance of its duties; and here we cannot resist quoting from the memoir formerly referred to, Mr. Charles's views and feelings on this interesting occasion: " I felt an earnest desire that the Lord would enable me to devote myself wholly to his service during the remainder of my days on earth, and was not a little impressed with the sense of the great importance of the charge I had taken upon me, and of my inability to discharge it faithfully. That solemn exhortation and charge in Acts xx. 28, sounds in my ears day and night. Is the church so dear and precious to Christ, that he purchased it with his most precious blood? What bowels of compassion and mercy then should I exercise towards every one, even the meanest individual in it! How solicitous should I be about their welfare, how anxious about their salvation! May God of his infinite goodness enable me to be faithful, and may the Spirit of Jehovah rest upon me for evermore." Acting under such views, Mr. Charles entered upon the performance of his duties, and officiated as curate in several parishes, till 1784. Such, however, was the hatred at this time manifested to the doctrines he preached, by those in power in the church, that he was forced to resign his charges one after another, and was at last literally driven to exercise his ministry beyond her communion. The detail of his life during this trying period is deeply interesting, and will amply repay an attentive perusal. His active mind would not allow him to be wholly unemployed. The ignorance which prevailed among the young people at Bala, Merionethshire, where he had now fixed his residence, excited his sympathy. He invited them to his house on the Sabbath evenings to catechise them, and give them religious instruction. His manner was peculiarly kind and affectionate, and the love and tenderness with which he addressed them, melted them into tears. His house soon became too small to contain those who attended, and he was offered the use of their chapel by the Calvinistic Methodists, who were then, and for a long time after, connected with the Established Church. This offer he gladly accepted, and instructed and catechised the large number of children who attended. This work was the delight of his heart, and was the commencement of Sabbath school instruction in that part of the country. Shortly after this, Mr Charles began preaching regularly in connection with the Whitefield or Calvinistic Methodists, and it was at this time that his active labours in Wales commenced. He was now about thirty years of age, and not a novice either in religion or in the ministry. Twelve years had elapsed since the time at which he dates the beginning of his acquaintance with the true nature of the Gospel, and he had now been more than seven years in the ministry. He had passed through a series of mental conflicts with the evil of his own heart not often experienced, and had also been favoured with comforting views of divine things not commonly enjoyed. The field of labour on which Mr. Charles now entered was very unpromising. True religion, says his biographer, had, for the most part, forsaken the country. Those who possessed a knowledge of the Gospel were few, when compared with the mass of the people around them, who were sunk to the lowest depths of ignorance and immorality. The Bible was almost an unknown book, and in many parishes, not even ten persons could be found capable of reading it. In the summer of 1785, Mr. Charles attended the Annual Association at Llangeitho, then the principal place of resort to all the religious people throughout the principality. He preached before the Association, and the great and venerable Rowlands formerly mentioned was one of his hearers. This aged servant of Christ had great penetration, and instantly perceived that Mr. Charles was no common man. His remark on the occasion was, "Charles is a gift from the Lord to North Wales;" and had he been a prophet, he could not have uttered a more correct prediction. God soon began to follow with a remarkable blessing, the labours of Mr. Charles. In September of the same year, he preached at Loufudr, Caernarvonshire. Many were deeply impressed during the discourse. No less apparent was the power which accompanied his preaching soon after, at an association held at Bontuchel, near Ruthin, Denbighshire. A divine unction seemed to accompany the word. Convictions of the strongest kind were produced. The most hardened sinners were broken down, and made to weep loudly, and to abhor themselves in dust and ashes." Many, depressed under a sense of their sinfulness, were made to rejoice in the salvation of their God, being filled "with joy unspeakable, and full of glory." The scene at times was most interesting and affecting : hundreds melted into tears ; some mourning with a godly sorrow for sin ; others weeping for joy, and exulting in a glorious Saviour ; some with their countenances betraying the deepest grief, becoming those who were crying out, "what must they do to be saved." The faces of others again, though bedewed with tears, were glistering with expressions of joy and thankfulness. These effects were produced, not by any fanciful or exaggerated statement, but by the words of truth and soberness ; and, no doubt, accompanied by the power and demonstration of the Spirit of God.

Mr C. had an active and inquisitive mind, always planning and contriving something to forward the interests of true religion. The present manner of exercising his ministry, afforded him opportunities of becoming acquainted with the condition of the country ; and the result of his inquiries disclosed a state of things most appalling. Ignorance of religion prevailed to an extent scarcely conceivable in a country professedly Christian. Having thus acquired a knowledge of the religious state of the country, he felt anxious to provide a remedy, and the plan he thought of, was the establishment of circulating schools, moveable from one place to another as circumstances required ; but Mr. Charles had two difficulties to surmount in the prosecution of his design,—to raise money to support the schools, and to procure teachers. We shall give the account of the commencement and prosecution of this benevolent undertaking in Mr. Charles's own words in writing to some friends on the subject :—

"In my travels through different parts of North Wales, about twenty-three years ago, I perceived that the state of the poor of the country in general, was so low as to religious knowledge, that in many parts not one person in twenty was capable of reading the Scriptures, and in some districts hardly an individual could be found who had received any instruction in reading. This discovery pained me beyond what I can express, and made me think seriously of some remedy, effectual and speedy, for the redress of this grievance. I accordingly proposed to a few friends to set a subscription on foot to pay the wages of a teacher, who was to be moved circuitously from one place to another ; to instruct the poor in reading, and in the first principles of Christianity by catechising them. This work began in the year 1785. At first only one teacher was employed. As the funds increased, so in proportion the number of teachers was enlarged, till they amounted to twenty. Some of the first teachers I was obliged to instruct myself ; and these afterwards instructed others sent them to learn to be schoolmasters."

Not content with imparting instruction to the young, Mr. Charles urged upon all of every age the duty of being able to read for themselves the word of God, and he had the gratification of seeing parents sitting down with their children in the same school, and learning to read that blessed book which maketh wise unto salvation. As to the progress of the schools, and the effects produced by them, we give the following quotation :—" The spirit of learning has rapidly spread among young people and children in large populous districts, where hitherto it had been wholly neglected. Their usual profanation of the Sabbath, in meeting for play, or in public-houses, has been forsaken, and the Sabbaths are now spent in the schools, or in religious exercises. We have also this year held associations of the different schools. They meet in some central place to be publicly catechised. On one occasion, the effect that followed an examination of these schools was very remarkable. In a town, which seemed to grow worse and worse, increasing daily in all kinds of wickedness, the people, young and old, running into all manner of excesses, especially at the annual wakes, Mr. Charles, lamenting this state of things, made up his mind to attempt to storm this stronghold of Satan. About two months before the wakes, he sent to the teachers of the Sabbath schools, requesting them to get the children to search the Bible for texts which prohibit directly or indirectly such evil practices as dancing, drunkenness, sensual indulgences, &c., and to commit them to memory, saying, that they might expect him there at the feast to catechise the children. The young people set to work, and there was a great deal of talk in the town and neighbourhood about the subject. When the time arrived, Mr. Charles went there, and most of the people of the place, led by curiosity in a great measure, went to hear what the children had to say on these subjects. The meeting began, as usual, with singing and prayer. Then Mr. C. began to ask them questions on the points given them to learn. Is drunkenness set forth as bad and sinful in Scripture? Yes, said one, and repeated these words, "Woe unto them that follow strong drink, that continue until night, until wine inflame them, and the harp and the viol, the tabret and the pipe, are in their feasts; but they regard not the work of the Lord, neither consider the operation of his hands," Isaiah v. 11, 12. In this way he proceeded with them concerning the other sins, and the answers were given with great propriety and seriousness. The people began to hold down their heads, and appeared to be much affected. Observing this, he addressed them in the kindest manner, and exhorted them by all means to leave off their sinful practices, to relinquish the works of darkness, to come to Christ, who was waiting to be gracious, to learn the word of God, after the example of their children, and to try to seek superior pleasures, and a better world. The effect was so great that all went home, and the houses of revelling were completely forsaken. The following day the harper was met going home by a person on the road, who, surprised to see him leaving the place so soon, asked him what was the reason, 'Some minister,' said he, 'has been catechising there, and persuaded the young people not to attend the feast.'" Such are some of the effects of these interesting schools, which, along with the faithful preaching of the Gospel, prepared the way for the great revival of religion which took place in North Wales, beginning in the year 1791, for the particulars of which, we again quote from Mr. Charles's Letters:—

" You inquire about the state of the churches in Wales. I have nothing but what is favourable to communicate. We had lately a very comfortable association at Pwllheli. Some thousands attended; more than ever was seen before. And here, at Bala, we have had a very great, powerful, and glorious outpouring of the Spirit on the people in general, especially on the children and young people. Scores of the wildest and most inconsiderate of young people of both sexes have been awakened. Their convictions have been very clear and powerful; and in some instances so deep as to bring them to the brink of despair. Their consolations have also been equally strong. If the Lord should be graciously pleased to continue the work, as it has prevailed some weeks past, the devil's kingdom will be in ruins in this neighbourhood. Ride on, ride on, thou King of glory, is the fervent cry of my soul, day and night. I verily believe that the Lord means to give the kingdom of darkness a dreadful shake; for he takes off its pillars. Those that were foremost in the service of Satan and rebellion against God, are now the foremost in seeking salvation through the blood of the Lamb. It is an easy work to preach the Gospel of the kingdom here at this time. Divine truths have their own infinite weight and importance on the minds of the people. Beams of divine light, together with divine irresistible energy, accompany every truth delivered. It is glorious to see how the stoutest hearts are bowed down and the hardest melted. I would not have been without seeing what I have lately seen, no, not for the world.

" These are the blessed things I have to relate to you, my dear brother, respecting poor Wales. The charity schools here are abundantly blessed. Children that were aforetime like jewels buried in rubbish, now appear with divine lustre and transcendent beauty. Little children from six to twelve years of age, are affected, astonished, and overpowered. Their young minds, day and night, are filled with nothing but soul-concerns. All I say is matter of fact. I have not exaggerated in the least degree, nor related more than a small part of the whole. The Lord hath done great things for us, and to him be all the praise."

One of the ministers of Edinburgh having seen this Letter, wrote Mr. Charles in March, 1792, mentioning the Revivals which took place in Scotland in 1742, and requesting further information, to which, Mr. Charles, in May of the same year, sent the following reply:—

" That it was the work of God I am not left to doubt in the least degree. It carries along with it every scriptural, satisfactory evidence that we can possibly desire; such as deep conviction of sin, of righteousness, and of judgment,—great reformation of manners,—great love for, and delight in, the Word of God, in prayer, in spiritual conversation, and divine ordinances. These, even in young persons, occupy the place and employ the time that was spent in vain diversions and amusements. No harps, but the golden harps, of which St. John speaks, have been played on in this neighbourhood for some months past. The craft is not only in danger, but entirely destroyed and abolished. The *little stone* has broken in pieces, and wholly destroyed these ensnaring hindrances.

" But I am far from expecting that all those who have experienced these impressions are savingly wrought upon and really converted. If that were the case, all the country must have been converted; for at one time there were but very few who had not felt awful impressions on their minds, producing foreboding fears respecting their future existence in another world. It was a most solemn time indeed! I never saw a livelier picture of the state of men's minds at the day of judgment, according to their respective conditions. That awful dispensation lasted but for a few weeks. But the ministration of the Word is still lively and powerful; and fresh awakenings take place, though not so numerous as at first. Perhaps it will not be known till the day of judgment how many of these new converts are actually brought into a state of salvation, nor who they are. But hitherto we have every reason to be thankful for the good progress they continue to make. Among so many there must be great variety; and we may have better hopes of some than others; but hitherto none have turned away from feeding beside the Shepherd's tents.

" As to the further spread of the work, the prospect in our country is in general very pleasing. In Caernarvonshire and Anglesea, the congregations are very numerous. Thousands flock together at the sound of the Gospel trumpet, and hear with great earnestness and attention. Awakenings also are frequent. The report of what had been going on in this place awakened the attention of the whole country, and filled the churches every where with the spirit of thanksgiving and prayer. The beginning was so glorious that I cannot think but that it precedes great things. The churches every where are prepared; they are praying; they are waiting and longing for His coming. He has indeed done already great things in this principality. Within these fifty years there have been five or six very great awakenings.

" Your saying that a similar work took place in your country about fifty years ago, has enkindled a spirit of prayer in me for the return of your jubilee. I am persuaded, that except we are favoured with frequent revivals, and a strong and powerful work of the Spirit, we shall in a great degree degenerate, and have only a 'name to live;' religion will lose its vigour; the ministry will hardly retain its lustre and glory, and iniquity will of course abound. I am far from supposing this to be the case in your country. I am only speaking of the thing itself. Scotland, I know, in ages past, has been a highly-favoured country. I hope it still continues so: but I am perfectly ignorant of the present state of religion in it. May the good Lord hasten that blessed time, when the kingdoms of the world shall become the kingdoms of the Lord and his Christ."

In January, 1794, in writing to the same clergyman, whose name we regret his biographer has not given, he thus further details the progress of the work. "In the course of last year, the almighty power of the Gospel has been most gloriously manifested in different parts of our country. There was a very general awakening through a very large and populous district of Caernarvonshire. In the space of three months, some hundreds were brought under concern about their souls. Oh! my dear Sir, it is a melodious sound, yes, in the ears of God himself, to hear poor perishing sinners crying out, 'what must we do to be saved?' The effects on the country at large are a general reformation of manners, the most diligent attention to the means of grace, private and public, and thirst after divine knowledge. Here at Bala, through mercy, we go on well, and have much cause for thankfulness, though not favoured with the wonderful scenes with which we were gratified two years ago. There is a work going on among us still, though not so powerfully as at the period alluded to. In some of the Schools we have had general awakenings among all the children. We take great care that the teachers be men of piety and of zeal, for the conversion of sinners. We have but one point in view in these institutions, that is the salvation of souls. We endeavour to set this point before them in all its infinite importance, as far surpassing all other matters whatever. This is what we aim to do ; but ah ! how little would all avail were it not for the powerful agency of the Holy Spirit. Blessed be God, we see him evidently and gloriously at work among us, never more so than at the present time, taking the country at large. Bless the Lord on our behalf, and pray for a continuance of his loving kindness."

The sentiments of the late Rev. John Newton of St. Mary, Woolnoth, London, respecting this revival, are very pleasing, bearing as they do, on revivals generally. It is contained in a Letter to the Edinburgh minister, so often referred to, and dated London, 20th February, 1792. "The revival at Bala demands thankfulness; the Lord, according to his sovereign pleasure, now and then vouchsafes such seasons of refreshment, as draw the attention of many. But hitherto they have been local and temporary. I remember one in Scotland, about fifty years ago, the most extensive I think took place in America, about the same time, and was first observed under Dr. Edwards' ministry at Northampton. There is generally much good done on such occasions of power, but we must not expect that every appearance will answer our wishes. There are many more blossoms in Spring than apples in the Autumn; yet we are glad to see blossoms, because we know that if there be no blossoms, there can be no fruit. Yet when sudden and general awakenings take place among people who are ignorant and unacquainted with scripture, they are more or less attended with blemishes and misguided zeal. The enemy is watchful to sow tares among the wheat. Thus it has always been. It was so in the Apostles' days, offences arise, and they who watch to find something at which they may stumble and cavil by the righteous judgment of God, have what they wish for. But they who love the Lord and have a regard for precious souls, will rejoice in the good that is really done, and can account for the occasional mixture from the present state of our nature. That the good work at Bala may flourish and extend to London and Edinburgh if the Lord pleases, is my sincere prayer, and I doubt not it is yours."

Mr. Charles continued his most useful labours in the vineyard for twenty years longer with great success. He established and conducted for several years a religious magazine for diffusing intelligence respecting the state of religion at home, and missionary operations abroad. He also assisted in the formation of the Bible Society, and in preparing a new edition of the Welsh Bible published by that Society. He closed a most laborious life in promoting the best interests of his countrymen, on the 5th October, 1814, in the 59th year of his age.

Thus we have given a brief but imperfect sketch of several of the instruments raised up by the great Head of the Church, for advancing the interests of vital religion in Wales; and although for the most part the statements have been more general in their character than could be wished, yet enough has been said to encourage Christians to the continued exercise of believing prayer "that God would arise and have mercy upon Zion, that the time to favour her, yea, the set time, may come."

REVIVALS OF RELIGION.

THE "spirit of slumber," which pervaded Scotland in the latter portion of the last century, exerted its most powerful influence over the whole of the north-west Highlands. Indeed the Reformation, in those districts, was nothing more than a change from the profession of one creed to that of another, according to the views of the proprietors of the soil. It was purely political; and partook of none of the intelligence, and preference of truth in opposition to papal ignorance and superstition, which distinguished that blessed era in the southern and north-eastern counties. Had a pious clergy succeeded their ghostly predecessors, the knowledge of the "letter" of the truth would, no doubt, have been imparted to the population of the interesting districts in question; and although they might, notwithstanding, have been left without any remarkable *revivals* of religion, the "gross darkness" which for so long a time prevailed would, in part at least, have been done away. This, however, was not the case : and there are parishes which, even up to the present date, have never, perhaps since the Gospel was first propagated, had the benefit of the pure preaching of the "glad tidings of salvation." Bibles, until very recently, there were none; and the power to read them, had they existed, was possessed by few of the common people, until the Gælic School Society commenced its operations. The instruction communicated by the parochial schools, was rigidly confined to English—in which course they were too long followed by those of the venerable Society for propagating Christian Knowledge, whose influence, however, was but partially extended to the region alluded to—and thus their united efforts are not much to be taken into account as affecting the moral character of the people—a fact well known to those who have come in contact with them, in the way of spiritual superintendence.

The more remote the Highland districts from the counties above referred to, the deeper the darkness ; and of these none perhaps, exceeded the northern portions of Skye—indeed the whole of that island. Many illustrations of this might be given if necessary ; we only remark, that what the common people were in point of intelligence, may be conceived when it is true, that after religion began to make some little progress, it was no uncommon thing for the better educated of the community gravely to maintain, that the Bible in use then was quite different from the one they had been accustomed to. When God therefore visited this island with the remarkable revival with which it was blessed, soon after the commencement of the present century, the sovereignty, as well as the power of divine grace, was thereby signally displayed. " He will have mercy on whom he will have mercy —and he will have compassion on whom he will have compassion."

Many years ago, and long before any awakening took place in Skye, a young girl, of little more than childish years, residing in a glen which, during the revival, was distinguished by much of divine power, became deeply impressed with the idea that God was not in her native isle. At the same time, she was overcome by the feeling, that she must go in pursuit of him where he was to be found. She accordingly stole away from her parents, and travelled across the country to the usual outlet by the ferry to the mainland. As she proceeded, she made no secret of the errand on which she had departed, and as her relations had taken up the opinion that she had become unsound in her mind, little attempt was made to recall her. So soon as she was out of Skye, she began to ask every passenger with whom she met, where she might find God, for that he was not in her country. She called at houses too by the way, asking direction in her uncommon inquiry. Pity and kind treatment marked the conduct of all towards her. Her question excited surprise ; but as her manner expressed sincerity and deep earnestness, every one answered her soothingly, and as unwilling to interfere with the hallucination under which they conceived she laboured. In this way she journeyed for days and weeks; but, though disappointed in every application for the knowledge which she sought, she did not desist. At length she reached the town of Inverness—often heard of, and which her youthful imagination had long pictured the centre of all that was good and valuable, as well as great. The first person whom she there met, and to whom she made application, was a pious lady, addressed by her on the street. She stopped her, and said in Gaelic: "I am come from Skye, where God is not—can you tell me where I shall find him?" The lady was struck not more with the unusual nature of the address, than the deep-toned earnestness and solemnity of her manner. Her first impression was that of all the others to whom the poor child had spoken by the way ; but she engaged in conversation with her, and became satisfied of her sanity. "Come with me," at last she said, " perhaps I can bring you to where you shall find God." She took her to her home. Next day was Sabbath. The wanderer accompanied her kind protector to the house of God. For the first time the Gospel was proclaimed in her hearing—it came "in demonstration of the Spirit and of power" to her soul. She was an awakened sinner, and soon became a happy convert—lived for many years in the lady's family—never again returned to Skye—married and settled in the parish of Croy, near Inverness, and was one of the most eminent Christians of her day. She lived long, and was greatly distinguished for her devotedness and fervency as a follower of the Lamb. Often have the pious in Skye said to each other: "Who can tell but the prayers of her who was led, by a way which she knew not, to the knowledge of the God of Abraham, may be receiving their answer in the great work which, in this dark place, he has been pleased to produce?" And who can tell? If the Lord prepares by his grace, those who plead with him—those who lay hold on his strength—will he not, in due time, answer them, and declare his faithfulness? Often, doubtless, were this good woman's earnest supplications offered up for her native isle; and if, though after a long time, the dayspring from on high did visit it—and the light which beams from Zion's hill, did shine into the vale where first she drew breath, who will say, but in granting this blessing, the hearer of prayer had regard to her request, and fulfilled the word of his promise, that the seed of Jacob seek him not in vain? No one can estimate how great a blessing it is to have a friend—a child of God—to pray for him: and no one can tell how valuable and important was the result, connected with the simple event now related, which separated an insignificant individual from her country and kindred that, far from her home, she might learn to pray to the living God, and that a long life should be passed in seeking light for those who sat in darkness, and times of refreshing for those who were perishing in a dry and barren wilderness.

In 1805, Mr. Farquharson, an itinerant preacher in the Independent connexion, first appeared in Skye. He was from Perthshire, where his ministrations had been much acknowledged; as indeed, they were wherever he proceeded in his labour of love. It is probable, that the "truth as it is in Jesus," had never before been publicly proclaimed in the island which he now visited. From the parochial pulpits, there is too much reason to fear, it did not go forth; and the remoteness of the district had hitherto precluded the visits of those not connected with the Church, who, towards the close of last century and beginning of the present, travelled over the country promulgating sound doctrine and, we believe, sincerely seeking the salvation of souls.

When Mr. Farquharson appeared in Skye, there is reason to believe, the state of religion was as unfavourable as it had ever been. The novelty of field-preaching on week days, as well as Sabbaths, by one who held no communion with the clergy. attracted the notice of the people, and they flocked in crowds to hear him. His sermons consisted of powerful and faithful testimonies against the abounding sins of the country, clear and energetic illustration of evangelical truth, solemn protests against the soul-destroying doctrine of justification by human merit, with affectionate and solemn warnings and invitations addressed to his hearers as lost sinners. His appeals excited great attention and produced no small inquiry among the people. But their external disadvantages were many—few could read, and scarcely any copies of the sacred volume were in their possession. In a population of many thousands, not above five or six New Testaments could be numbered, and their value had never been appreciated. Still the preaching of the Gospel continued. In Portree and Snizort, Kilmuir, Diurnish, and Bracadale, Mr. Farquharson itinerated for a considerable time—the people heard, and deep seriousness marked their whole demeanour under the word of life.

At this time, there lived in the parish of Portree, a person named Donald Munro. In childhood he had been the victim of small pox, by which he had lost his sight. To gain a livelihood he had learned to play the violin; and being naturally of a pleasant disposition, this quality, with his musical talent, made him a general favourite. The calamity of his blindness engaged the sympathy of all, and his other qualifications secured their patronage. It was thought that the office of Catechist in the parish, to which a small salary was attached, might be superadded to his professional character with advantage to his circumstances. The inconsistency, if observed, was overlooked, and the benevolence implied in making a provision for Donald, concealed the incongruity of a blind fiddler being also a parochial catechist. The minister favoured him—the people were pleased with the arrangement, and a retentive memory enabling him to master the questions of the Shorter Catechism, and a few chapters in the New Testament, his qualifications for the office to which he was promoted were held to be complete. How often are we made to know, as the sequel of this man's history will illustrate, that "God's ways are not our ways"—that they are "past finding out." "for he giveth not account of any of his matters."

Donald's official character led him to hear Mr. Farquharson —for where religious exercises, extra-ministerial, were held, there he conceived it his duty to be. Hundreds and hundreds had come to listen to the word of salvation; but, although serious attention was given, the preacher seemed to have "run in vain and laboured in vain." The Spirit was not poured out from on high, and no "blade" of heavenly growth was yet discoverable in that dry place. Nevertheless, God had sent him; and, although he was not, himself, to be the direct instrument of an abundant harvest, like the prophets of old, he was made the medium of the " unction from the Holy One," to another who was raised up to show how "the weak things of the world are made to confound the mighty—and base things of the world and things that are despised, yea, and things which are not, chosen to bring to nought things that are, that no flesh should glory in his presence." "To me he was a messenger from God," declared Donald Munro many years after; and although in his Christian charity he expressed an opinion, that one or two besides were converted by his means, no evidence exists that faithful Farquharson's mission had any other direct fruit than that of the conversion of this remarkable man. He soon after emigrated to America, and his ministrations had no further connexion with the revival which took place in Skye.

The Catechist of Portree was no longer a pluralist. He had "got new views," to use his own language, of "Scripture truths, of himself, and of the practices of the inhabitants of his island;" and the light which had been given to him he did not put "under a bushel." His official situation afforded him opportunities of speaking in the name of Jesus; and, before he had been himself a convert for a year, he was made the instrument of turning three or four from the error of their ways to the faith and obedience of the glorious Gospel.

But the great awakening did not take place now, nor for a few years after this; nevertheless as the events which follow were connected with that manifestation of divine grace and power, and as they illustrate the ways of God's providence in promoting his purposes of love towards sinners, they are here recorded.

In the first place, a prayer meeting was established. This was in Snizort, the neighbouring parish to Portree. A very few only attended at its establishment; but, in course of time, the numbers increased. The prejudice against it was strong; for nothing of the kind had ever before been heard of in the country, and an innovation of so marked a character was not readily tolerated. But it grew in popularity; and by its means many were induced to attempt to call on the name of the Lord. For two years it flourished. At the end of that time a Baptist preacher appeared in the country. The members of the meeting heard, and some were drawn after him. Eleven were baptized by him—division ensued, and the prayer meeting was in a short time finally dissolved.

In the next place, soon after the institution of this meeting, it pleased the Lord to bring "out of darkness into marvellous light" one of the ministers in the neighbourhood. The tleman referred to was the late Mr. Martin, then of Kilmuir, and latterly of the parish of Abernethy. The change in his doctrine, as well as life and conversation, soon attracted notice, and he was sought unto by those in the country who, by this time, had themselves tasted that the Lord is gracious. The cause of the prayer meeting was espoused by him; and as, even men who knew not the saving power of the Gospel in their own experience, esteemed him for his virtues, his countenance given it, secured either their neutrality or favour. As a minister, he was instant in season and out of season; reproving, rebuking, exhorting with all long-suffering and doc trine. The usual result followed—a desire among his parishioners to search the Scriptures, to see that the things which he declared were so. But the sacred volume was awanting—and no supply was at hand to meet the demand which the preaching of Christ crucified by this good man had produced. What might have followed so prosperous a state of outward privilege no one can say. A very few, it is believed, were during the short period of Mr. Martin's living ministry, savingly impressed; but as he removed from the island in about two years after the change in his own character, and the Gospel ceased to be proclaimed—although he left a pious Catechist behind him—no further additions of such as were "ordained to eternal life," were at that time made to the "Church of the living God."

And here we may be permitted to remark, how serious a consideration it may be for a minister of the Gospel to remove, under whatever solicitations, from a sphere where indications may be perceived of an incipient work of grace, such as a few years after distinguished this part of Skye. That Mr. Martin should be exposed to much that might harass his spirit, under his change of views and character, in the place where his lot was cast—that "living godly in Christ Jesus" he should suffer persecution—may be readily believed, as the experience of another, but more undaunted "fellow-servant" subsequently attested; but surely here was an opportunity to "endure the cross, and despise the shame," connected with the prospect of honouring his Master and promoting his cause, such as does not often occur, and which, not being embraced, is seldom a second time offered to any man. It cannot be wondered that Mr. Martin, as we have heard, should in after years have felt and lamented his error.

It has been stated, that he left behind him, in the parish of Kilmuir, a pious Catechist. This individual also acted as schoolmaster. But besides his services, the parish now enjoyed the benefit of those of Donald Munro, who had been discharged from his office in Portree, and was therefore not confined in his labours to that locality. Under their direction and conduct, meetings, subsequently to the dissolution of the prayer meeting, were regularly held in the parish, attended by large multitudes; and much interest, appareatly, was taken in the things which belonged to their souls. This state of matters, however, lasted not long. The new incumbent did not walk in the steps of his predecessor. The Catechist, disgusted with the new order of things, left the country; and Donald Munro stood single-handed without even the weight which his former official name afforded. He did not, however, cease his efforts; and, though under many inconveniences, this good man persevered in holding the meetings, encouraged by the great numbers who came desirous to listen to the word of life.

But the Lord raised up a new friend to the cause in the person of the late Mr. John Shaw, who, about this time, was appointed minister of Bracadale, a parish in the neighbourhood, and situated in the same district of country. He had previously been the assistant of the minister of Diurnish, a parish also in this district; but, acting there in an inferior capacity, his influence, until now, had not been efficiently exerted. He was a holy and humble man—little acquainted with the ways of the world, and naturally little qualified to withstand its opposition, directed, whether insidiously or in open violence, against the interests of Sion. But, whatever his failing in this, his heart trembled for the ark of the Lord—its safety was the object of his deepest solicitude, and the theme of his importunate and constant prayers. He was consequently the friend of the friends of Christ, and, few and despised as they were in Skye, he constituted a rallying point and counseller, whose unwavering faithfulness, at least, seldom failed them in whatever emergency.

Mr. Shaw secured for his parish the benefit of Society teachers, all of whom were godly men—one from the Society for propagating Christian Knowledge—another from the Gælic School Society—and a third from the Inverness Education Society; by whose means a knowledge of the truths of the Scripture was extensively communicated. And not least in importance, as preparing the way for the work which the Lord was about to perform in this hitherto dark corner of the Church, the minister of Bracadale introduced to the country Mr. M‘Donald of Urquhart, "whose praise is in the gospel throughout all the churches," and whose rousing appeals to the assembled multitudes who congregated to hear him, caused " no small stir about that way."

It was about the year 1812 that the *awakening*, properly so called, had its commencement—about seven years after Mr. Farquharson first preached in Skye. It began in the parish of Kilmuir, of which Mr. Martin had been minister; and where Donald Munro's services had been most uniformly bestowed and best appreciated. As there can be no doubt that the meetings held under his management were the means 'specially employed in the work, it may be proper to state the mode in which the services on those occasions were conducted. We are not here to defend the *regularity* of these meetings, if this be impugned. It pleased the Lord to bless them ; and, considering the circumstances which gave them birth and caused their continuance, he will be a bold man who maintains that they ought to have been suppressed or that they are now to be condemned.

The services, on the solemn aud happy occasions of which we speak, began with praise and prayer; which were sometimes repeated in course of the occasion, and always concluded the duties for the time. The reading of the Scripture followed the opening of the meeting—large portions of which were read aloud without note or comment. The works of such authors as were to be had in Gælic came next—viz., translations of Alleine's Alarm, Boston's Fourfold State, Baxter's Call, Bunyan, Willison, Gray and Edwards. Then a passage of the word of God was selected for exposition. Munro, usually, had this part of the service allotted to him : but although few, when he was present, were willing to occupy the place which became him so well, others also, at times, opened up the truths contained in the passage thus commented on. It has already been noted that Donald was a blind man : but, he required the aid of no reader. His memory was stored with the Scriptures; and he had become, literally, a living concordance. Whole chapters could be recited by him without the commission of the slightest error. References, for illustration, were made with a precision which never betrayed, in a single instance, those who followed him in his exposition by turning to the passages. His style of address was solemn and deeply impressive—the effect being not a little heightened by the visitation of Providence which had made him an object of sympathy to all, connected with the evidence in him of the riches of His grace who had come

> ——"To clear the inward sight;
> And on the eyeballs of the blind
> To pour celestial light."

He spoke as one "scarcely saved"—"a brand plucked out of the burning"—lately "dead in trespasses and in sins ;" but to whom "the grace of the Lord had been exceeding abundant," and who now stood among those of his own country and kindred who knew his "manner of life from his youth," apparently by divine commission, to warn them to flee from the wrath to come; and to proclaim the truth, worthy of all acceptation, that Christ Jesus came into the world to save sinners, of whom he had been chief A holy unction characterised—as a sound judgment ruled—all that he said: for his words were weighed in the balance of the sanctuary and were not found wanting. To witness his appearance on the occasions alluded to—if the heart were not melted—was sure to disarm prejudice; and even bitter enemies, whilst they condemned the proceedings, acknowledged that Donald was a good man—honest and sincere in the cause in which he was embarked.

Three times, every sabbath day, the meetings were held—in the open fields—in barns—or under such shelter as circumstances required and as at the time could be commanded. But not on the Lord's-day only: one stated meeting was held, weekly, at Donald's residence, on another day; and besides this, he travelled to other points in the country round, so that he was rarely disengaged.

Great power followed. When this came, the effects were striking in the highest degree; and filled Munro and the other leaders with adoring wonder. That it was the Lord's doing, not man's, soon became so evident that they were made to feel, and exulted to acknowledge, that they were not to be accounted of, and not worthy to be named in connection with the glorious manifestation which it pleased the Most High to vouchsafe of his redeeming love. "What are we and what is our Father's house!" was the language of their hearts while they contemplated the effects of the irresistible power now savingly exerted. It was a common thing, as soon as the Bible was opened, after the preliminary services, and just as the reader began, for great meltings to come upon the hearers. The deepest attention was paid to every word as the sacred verses were slowly and solemnly enunciated. Then the silent tear might be seen stealing down the rugged, but expressive, countenances turned upon the reader—the convulsive and half-suppressed sigh might next be heard—female sobbings followed—and, after a little, every breast was heaving under the unaccountable agitation which moved the spirits of the assembled multitudes. "The wind bloweth where it listeth, and thou hearest the sound thereof, but canst not tell whence it cometh or whither it goeth; so is every one who is born of the Spirit."

Sometimes those affected cried aloud; but this was not common: at other times they threw themselves upon the grass, in the utmost distress, and "wept bitterly." A spirit of prayer and supplication was granted, in a remarkable degree, both upon the leaders of the meetings and upon the people. After the services for the occasion, at any time, were concluded, they were to be seen, in all directions, on their knees, or stretched along upon the ground, calling upon His name with whom is "the residue of the Spirit." An insatiable desire to hear the Scriptures read and opened prevailed; and no length of service fatigued during those days of life and power.

Hours passed insensibly and the night was often "far spent" ere "note was made of time." The usual seasons for food were forgotten; and even necessary nourishment was sometimes neglected. The redemption of the soul is indeed precious. When the eyes are enlightened to perceive this truth, and the conscience is awakened, under the operation of the Holy Spirit, to testify the fearfulness of coming short of the great salvation; and when this occurs, not to an isolated individual, but to a multitude circumstanced, in all respects, as those of whom we now speak, who can wonder that such appearances, as have been described, should be exhibited—that such results should follow; nay, who that knows the word of God and the mind of man, but might expect that such occurrences should take place?

We have called those occasions *happy*. They were truly so; for there is no joy like that which is felt when a sinner, melted under a sense of sin and of the mercy of God, learns to weep from "godly sorrow" and a blessed persuasion that everlasting love is manifested towards him in the dealings with his soul which he experiences—when at one and the same time "repentance towards God and faith towards the Lord Jesus Christ" are produced within him by a power which he knows is divine. One striking trait, accordingly, in the character of the meetings was the life felt and manifested *in singing the praises of God*. The assembled multitudes engaged in the duty as with "one heart and one soul;" and often seemed as if they knew not how to stop. The utmost cordiality and brotherly love prevailed—every man feeling his heart more tenderly drawn out to his neighbour—and such as were savingly affected experiencing a holy influence leading them to testify for Christ, in the house, and by the way, in private conversation and by a devoted public profession.

For about two years the awakening was general. As already stated, it began in the parish of Kilmuir. Snizort next enjoyed the life-giving influence—then Bracadale, and finally Diurnish—all contiguous parishes. Wherever Donald Munro proceeded the effects described followed; and for a time, it was estimated, three or four individuals were savingly converted at every meeting where he presided. Not only so; but when these converts engaged in spiritual exercises throughout the country—for they often came from a distance, and returned to their remote homes laden with the "unsearchable riches of Christ"—great power accompanied their services. It was a "time of refreshing from the presence of the Lord" and by every event connected with it he forcibly announced to all: "Not by might nor by power but by my Spirit."

The effects were two-fold—of a *primary* or direct, and of a *secondary* or indirect, character.

The primary effects were the genuine conversion of many sinners to the knowledge and obedience of the truth as it is in Jesus. In such a matter it is difficult, and may be dangerous, to speak of numbers : but it is well known that, during the general awakening, several hundreds were brought " from darkness to light and from the power of Satan to God." The genuineness of their conversion was evidenced by the change of life which accompanied their profession. Persons who had openly served sin, with their whole heart, did truly abandon it, embraced the cause of godliness, and walked, as those of them who still survive do, so as to " adorn the doctrine of God their Saviour by a life and conversation becoming it in all things. Some who had been noted for wickedness became eminent as Christians ; and until this day they labour in the vineyard, in their various stations, as " servants who need not to be ashamed." Those are not, in any case, the results of a vain enthusiasm, any more than the fruits of the day of Pentecost were the effect of " new wine :" but " mockers" now judge by the same rule, as they did then, being blinded by the same evil influence.

Among the secondary effects may be stated, first, the suppression of the openly sinful practices common in the country As the image of Dagon fell mutilated before the ark of the Lord, so did they before the Divine power now present in the district where they had prevailed. Those practices were no longer in repute, but discarded and abandoned by such, even, as were still secretly "joined to their idols." Whilst the devil was certainly *cast out* of many " by the finger of God," so that he should never return to find a resting place in them again—he also *went out* of many more ; and, for a time, the " house was swept and garnished."

In the next place, a large body was formed whose religion, instead of being a reflexion of the image of Christ, was no more than a reflexion of that of his people—the work in whom was not of God but of man. They constituted the tares among the wheat—the chaff among the true grain—the growth of the rocky ground contrasted with that of the good soil. They attached themselves to the others—appeared under the same circumstances, and thus, as in all revivals which have occurred in the various periods of the Church's history, offences, in course of time, came. These we believe were less numerous and momentous than the hatred of enemies represented them ; and probably might have been made less of, but for the anxiety of the real friends of Christ to vindicate his holy work from the imputation thrown on it from such a cause. They might have remembered that the existence of uch offences most truly declared the genuineness of the work of God among them; for where the good seed is made to take root, there the enemy will come and sow the evil '

In the third place, there followed from this awakening that abandonment of ordinances, as administered by the parochial clergy, which at present attracts the eyes of the supreme Church court to Skye and the adjacent districts. All the professors of religion—both real converts and others—remained devotedly attached to the national establishment, and resisted efforts made to draw them aside—in which mind they continue. But the evident and striking countenance granted to the *meetings* attracted the people to them, and secured their reverence for their services. The churches were, in consequence, very much forsaken. In these circumstances, the clergy began to refuse sealing ordinances to those who did not hear them; and, on the other hand, the "professors" lifted their protest against the clergy by refusing to accept ordinances as by them administered—Mr. Shaw being the only minister excepted, at that time, from the application of this rule. Hence, especially from this latter cause, it soon ceased to be matter of reproach to live in the non-enjoyment of the ordinances. More than this, it came to be counted an evidence of seriousness not to apply to the clergy—or a mark of carelessness and irreligion when application was made. And thus have we, in the bosom of the Church, the anomalous state of things of a large body of professing Christians, distinguished for the fervency of their piety, the purity of their lives, and the warmth of their attachment to her constitution, still maintaining their union with us under the deprivation of ordinances which they earnestly long for—receiving them, when permitted to do so, from ministers whom they approve and with whom, they conceive, they can hold Christian communion—and justifying separation. not from the Church, but from her ordinances, on the ground of their alleged prostitution by those who ought to be the guardians of their purity! This is not the place to discuss a question beset with many difficulties; but those who seek the true reformation of our national Sion, throughout her whole extent, will do well to pause ere they condemn so many of the "excellent of the earth" who, under much obloquy, have never let down their solemn protest, raised against abuses which they declare exist—whether more in Skye than elsewhere they know not—nor abandoned their pledged attachment to the Church of their fathers.

A few additional particulars must conclude this narrative. The good work related above was not hindered by any divisions. Enemies attempted to take advantage of the offences alluded to; which, however, but the more closely united the friends of truth: and as all were of one mind on the question regarding the ordinances, neither did this oppose any obstacle to the progess of the Word of Life.

We have stated that the parish of Diurnish was the most lately visited by the Divine influence. The awakening there took place a few years after the general revival in the country, and also by means of the meetings already described. The same effects, both as to external appearances and permanent good, followed in the one as in the other; and a great number, for the extent of the population, were turned unto the Lord. The desire to hear, and be benefited by, the word of salvation equalled now what existed in the earlier revival; and it was often a stirring sight to witness the multitudes assembling during the dark winter evenings—to trace their progress, as they came in all directions across moors and mountains, by the blazing torches which they carried to light their way to the places of meeting. The word of the Lord was precious in those days; and personal inconvenience was little thought of when the hungering soul sought to be satisfied.

The awakening now, as during the period of the greater effusion of the Spirit, was principally confined to those not much advanced in life—of the age of *fifteen*, and under, to *thirty*, both married and unmarried. But there were some striking exceptions to this rule on both occasions. One man, *eighty years of age*, was brought under great concern, lived a few years as a professed Christian and died, it is believed, in the Lord. A still more wonderful instance of the power of Divine grace was afforded in the case of a poor man, residing in the parish of Bracadale, above *one hundred years old*, who, in the judgment of charity, passed from death to life; having, from being ignorant and unholy, renounced his dependence on a covenant of works, and embraced the faith which purifies the heart and overcomes the world. The conversion of an idiot, or rather half-witted person, who afterwards emigrated with his relations to America, constituted another triumph of that grace which was so bountifully communicated in this hitherto barren wilderness. But time would fail to enumerate all the instances of this kind which occurred—including some, of persons little known, during their life, to be more than mere professors, who on their death-bed evinced the reality of the change that had been wrought on their souls. These are mentioned as illustrative of the sovereignty of God in the communications of his grace; and to encourage all who plead for them to remember that with him nothing is impossible —that he doth "wonderful things," and that his "counsels of old are faithfulness and truth."

In 1823, Mr. Shaw died; but the Lord had prepared one to do more than fill his place, in the person of Mr. Roderick M'Leod, who was appointed to succeed him in Bracadale. As a missionary in the neighbourhood, he had for a few years filled the office, without possessing the spirit or doing the work of an evangelist; but when thus "far off," it pleased

God to "call him by his grace, and to reveal his Son in him'
—so preparing and qualifying him to preach the "glorious
gospel." With his change of views and practice, as a minister
of the New Testament, he adopted the sentiments, prevalent
among the religious in the country, on the question regarding
the ordinances. His unflinching adherence to these, and a
consequently unusual strictness in the rule of admission, soon
involved him in troubles in the church courts, whilst it en-
deared him to all those in the country who had turned from
their idols to serve the living God. If any one thing could
have succeeded in separating for ever from our church this
valuable body of devoted adherents, it would have been the
deposition of this estimable man. Let us hope that the days
have gone by when such a risk might exist, nay, let us hope
that the time has come for the calm discussion of the principle of such vital importance to the interests of true religion,
for which he has so long contended.

Under Mr. M'Leod s ministry the good work was prolonged,
and, from time to time, through his instrumentality, many
were "added to the church of such as should be saved." A
door was still kept open for Mr. M'Donald of Urquhart, whose
apostolic visits continued to be regularly paid, and whose
faithful ministrations, during the whole progress of the work,
had been evidently acknowledged. Still more recently, another door was opened for him in Snizort, where Mr.M'Lachlan,
now of Cawdor, during a short ministerial course, zealously
preached the doctrine of the cross, and did not run in vain.

In 1830, Donald Munro died—a man highly honoured of
the Lord, and whose memory will be had in everlasting remembrance. It is impossible to reflect on his career without
being impressed with the truth that God is "no respecter of
persons," and that the distinctions, of which men are apt to
make so much, are often lightly set by of him. He can
choose his instruments from the most unlikely materials, and,
in performing his works of wonder, strikingly prove that "the
excellency of the power is of himself." He once selected a
child of tender years, through whom to speak to his people,
passing by a regularly appointed and aged servant; and not
more forcibly did he then announce, than he has done
among us, by the history of Donald Munro: "Them that
honour me I will honour, and they that despise me shall be
lightly esteemed."

This good man's services, although principally confined to
Skye, were not exclusively so. He sometimes visited the
mainland, especially on sacramental occasions ; but wherever
he proceeded the same holy influence was made to accompany
him, and the Lord honoured him as the means of promoting
his cause. A little anecdote, well known, will illustrate his
zeal and manner of proceeding during such solemn occasions

as we refer to. In this district of the Highlands, immense numbers from incredibly remote points assemble to the ordinance of the Supper, where faithful preaching or esteemed ministers are expected. They are usually accommodated at night in barns or large outhouses—the males occupying one department of the building, the females the other. A stranger who had n ver heard of Donald came to attend, on an occasion, at Lochcarron, during the ministry of the late Mr. Lachlan M'Kenzie, a man most eminent among his own people in his day and generation. The stranger had his bed allotted him in a large barn with a multitude accommodated in the same way. During the darkness of the night, he was aroused from his slumbers by a voice calling aloud "awake, awake!" The summons seemed to be obeyed, as if expected, judging by the movement which he perceived all around him. He then heard: "Let us sing to the praise of God," pronounced by the same voice. Several verses were distinctly enunciated amidst the darkness and the stillness of the night. They were sung, each line being regularly announced, with thrilling effect. Prayer was then offered up, the stranger perceiving all his fellow lodgers on their knees, and instinctively following their example. This duty ended, and a long portion of Scripture was distinctly pronounced. He was amazed; but much more was this the case when he listened to a striking and powerful exposition, with references to other scriptures, in proof or in illustration of doctrine, concluding with an irresistible appeal to the consciences of all who were present. It is not said that the stranger had "come to scoff"—but it is to be feared an idle curiosity, which too often guides many to such places, had led him thither: there is reason to believe, however, that he "remained to pray." The Lord had conducted him by a way which he knew not, when He directed his steps to the place to which he had come—He had touched his heart— and, from that day forth, this wanderer on the mountains of vanity, sought Sion with his face thitherward.

It only remains to be added that the meetings are still maintained in Skye, and that they prosper, through the blessing of God. Donald Munro has several worthy successors— places of assembly have been erected, and, from time to time, the "good Shepherd," by means of the services there engaged in, brings home some lost sheep, and feeds those who are already in the fold. In any parish in which the privilege of faithful and acceptable preaching in the church is enjoyed, the meetings are not held on the Sabbath, except in districts so remote as to preclude the possibility of attending there But in all the parishes which enjoyed the divine influence they are maintained on week days; the Sabbath being likewise appropriated in cases where the views of the ministers do not accord with those of the large body who adhere to the meetings. The attachment to the established church, on the part of this body, remains unaltered, whilst they continue to long for the time when the Lord will again beautify his Sion by reviving his work in midst of the years, and by sending times of refreshing from his presence throughout her whole extent.

The preceding narrative may well encourage all who pray for Jerusalem to continue instant in that duty—to wait patiently for Him, who will come and not tarry, and who is to be enquired of to do for Israel the good thing which he has purposed. It forcibly teaches also that we are not to despise the day of small things. To the eye of sense how hopeless was the cause of religion in Skye, when Munro stood alone there, friends as yet being few, and opponents many. Yet how striking at last was the testimony given to the persevering faithfulness of that humble man, who went out without the camp, bearing the reproach of Christ, and though he had little to lose, willingly suffered the loss of what he had, to follow Him. May every one who loves the Lord Jesus hear and obey the commandment: "Go thou and do likewise.'

The divine *sovereignty*, manifested in the work in Skye, ought to give encouragement to those who long for such manifestations of grace as were there afforded. No circumstances can be so hopeless as to justify a cessation of diligence in the use of such means as are ordinarily employed by the eternal Spirit, in his work, or to warrant us in saying that his day of power is not to come with its many blessings. On the contrary there is every thing in the Word and in his dealings with the church, as the foregoing narrative illustrates, to animate us in the exercise of increased faith, and a more lively hope, even as to situations where the darkness is deepest and the "spirit of slumber," the most profound. Let us therefore "gird up the loins of our mind, and hope to the end for the grace that is to be brought unto us at the revelation of Jesus Christ.

REVIVALS OF RELIGION.

No. XI.

KILSYTH, 1839,

Being the Substance of a Statement by the Rev. Mr. Burns, Minister of the Parish, drawn up at the request of the Presbytery of Glasgow, with Additions.

I WAS admitted to the charge of this parish on the 19th April, 1821, on which I entered "in weakness, and in fear, and in much trembling."* I saw a beautiful valley before me, like that of Sodom, rich and well watered; but, alas! it bore too close a resemblance to it also in its spiritual and moral aspect. Yet there were several Lots, yea Jacobs, among them, who prayed and wrestled for the return of the time of revival. This was often referred to in the prayers of my predecessor, and familiar to the ears of our people, who seemed to think it an honour to have their fathers' names and sepulchres thus built up and honoured, while they, alas! followed not their example.

A visitation of every family in a parish, after a minister's induction, is generally an important event in its history. Nothing could have been more kind than the reception I received from all classes and denominations, and which has met me ever since in my annual rounds. The appearance, too, at church, and the solemnity and prayers *at funerals*, struck me as indicative of more of a spirit of religion than I had anticipated: but these good symptoms were overbalanced by the appalling number who attended no place of worship, and by the woful prevalence of intemperance, and the lightness with which that vice seemed to be regarded, even by religious professors. I was struck with the meaning of our Saviour's words, "Because iniquity shall abound, the love of many waxeth cold."

There were four or five prayer meetings at that time in the *whole* parish : one of these, composed of the session members, had continued ever since the days of Robe. In 1823, classes on week-day evenings, for youth of both sexes from 14 to 20 years, were opened by myself. Four of the elders, who are now so active in the cause of revival, were members of the young men's class. Of late years a great increase in numbers and efficiency has taken place in the Sabbath schools; and in 1826, a most important improvement took place in the mode of parochial teaching. *The mind and heart* were daily plied with the lessons of *heavenly* as well as

---

* 1 Cor. ii, 3—my first text on Sabbath, the 21st April.

secular wisdom. In 1829, however, there were frightful out-breakings of wickedness, arising out of drunken quarrels. A day was set apart (January, 1830) for fasting and prayer on this account, and the reasons thereof set forth by a memorial from the Kirk Session. It was very solemnly observed, and was followed by an evident blessing. In 1832, the cholera visited this country. We saw a dark cloud discharging itself on the neighbouring town of Kirkintilloch; and our people seemed to reason with themselves, "whether this comes from east or west, whether from natural or moral causes, *we* may be assured of a visit of this dire calamity." (Yet it never actually came to us!) We had prayer meetings weekly in town and the two Baronies, which were flocked to by many, anxious that they might not die unprepared. The panic soon subsided, and the prayer meetings were thinned. I see it marked in my day-book, May 13, 1832, "Intimated prayer meetings for *revival of religion.*" Several lectures were given on the subject: at the same time commenced the monthly tract distribution, and exertions to arrest the tide of intemperance, and the conducting of funerals without any other service excepting a prayer. In March, 1836, after the communion, a prayer meeting was held in the church, especially for revival, addressed by the Rev. Mr. Walker of Muthil, who had preached on the subject on the Friday before, after which the prayer meetings in dwelling-houses were considerably increased in number, and in attendance—all in connexion with the Church. The Methodists had been for some years more or less active, both in the town and in the East Barony, and had roused not a few careless individuals; and the members of the Relief set about similar meetings. Sabbath evening lectures, of a very plain and familiar character, have been more or less resorted to, but regularly for three seasons; and have been mentioned by several individuals as the means of first impressing their hearts. A goodly number of poor people came out to these evening sermons, who could not be brought to attend on the ordinary services. Prayer meetings have been referred to by many as the means of their first serious thought; and sermons delivered in the church-yard last summer, by Mr. Somerville of Anderston, and by myself, have been often mentioned as having been blessed to awakening and enlivening. Nine months ago, a new missionary meeting begun, which interested many of our people. Still, after all these and other symptoms of good, it was not till Tuesday, the 23rd July, that a decided and unquestionable religious revival took place. We may well say of the amazing scene we have witnessed, "When the Lord turned our captivity we were as men that dreamed." We have, as it were, been awakened from a dream of a hundred years.

The communion had been, as usual, upon the third Sal

bath, and 21st day. Intimation had been made upon the Saturday, that the minister would wish to converse with such persons as were under religious concern, inasmuch as two or three had previously called upon that errand. The effect was that several other individuals did come to converse. The Monday evening was the half-yearly general meeting of our Missionary Society, when a sermon was delivered by Dr. Burns of Paisley—text, Isaiah, lii, 1 : " Awake," &c. It was intimated that Mr. William C. Burns, who had preached several times with much power during the solemnity, would address the people of Kilsyth next day, if the weather proved favourable, in the open air, the object being to get those to hear the word who could not be brought out in the ordinary way. It was known, too, that he was very shortly to leave this place for Dundee, and probably soon to engage in missionary labours in a distant land. The day was cloudy and rainy. The crowd, however, in the Market Place was great; and, on being invited to repair to the church, it was soon crowded to an overflow—the stairs, passages, and porches, being filled with a large assemblage of all descriptions of persons in their ordinary clothes. The prayer was solemn and affecting; the chapter read without any comment was Acts, ii. The sermon proceeded from Psalm cx, 3, " Thy people shall be willing in the day of thy power." Throughout the whole sermon there was more than usual seriousness and tenderness pervading the hearers ; but it was towards the close, when depicting the remarkable scene at Kirk of Shotts, on the Monday after the communion there, 1630, when, under the preaching of Mr. John Livingstone, a native of Kilsyth, 500 were converted,* that the emotions of the audience became too strong to be suppressed. The eyes of most of the audience were in tears ; and those who could observe the countenances of the hearers expected half an hour before, the scene which followed. After reciting Mr. Livingstone's text, Ezekiel, xxxvi, " A new heart will I give," &c., and when pressing upon his hearers the all-important concern of salvation, while, with very uncommon pathos and tenderness, he pressed immediate acceptance of Christ, each for himself—when referring to the affecting and awful state, in which he dreaded the thought of leaving so many of them whom he now saw probably for the last time—when, again and again, as he saw his words telling on the audience, beseeching sinners, old and young, to embrace Christ and be saved—when he was at the height of his appeal, with the words, " *no cross no crown,*"— then it was that the emotions of the audience were most overpoweringly expressed. A scene which scarcely can be described took place. I have no doubt, from the effects which have followed, and from the very numerous references to this

* See the Narrative of this Revival in No. IV of this Series.

day's service, as the immediate cause of their remarkable change of heart and life, that the convincing and converting influence of the Holy Spirit was at that time most unusually and remarkably conveyed. For a time the preacher's voice was quite inaudible; a psalm was sung tremulously by the precentor, and by a portion of the audience, most of whom were in tears. I was called by one of the elders to come to a woman who was praying in deep distress; several individuals were removed to the session-house, and a prayer meeting was immediately commenced. Dr. Burns, of Paisley, spoke to the people in church, in the way of caution and of direction, that the genuine, deep, inward working of the Spirit might go on, not encouraging animal excitement.

The church was dismissed after I had intimated that we were ready to converse with all who were distressed and anxious, and that there would be a meeting again in the evening for worship at six o'clock. We then adjourned to the vestry and session-house, which were completely filled with the spiritually-afflicted, and a considerable time was occupied with them. Several of the distressed were relieved before we parted. These were persons believed to be Christians, but who were not before this rejoicing in hope. Others continued for days in great anxiety, and came again and again; but are now, generally speaking, in a peaceful and hopeful state, and have been conversing with a view to admission to the Lord's table.

In the evening the church was again crowded to excess. Mr. Lyon of Banton lectured on the parable of the prodigal son, and Mr. William C. Burns preached from Matth. xviii, 3, "Except ye be converted," &c. The impression was deepened; but there was no great excitement, the aim of the preacher being to forward a genuine work of the Spirit.* A great many came to the manse to speak about their souls. Evening meetings in the church were continued without intermission, and even in the mornings occasionally. Our hands were full, but the work was precious, and often delightful. Our elders and praying men were, and still are, very useful in aiding us. He who was honoured as the chief instrument of the awakening was earnestly sought out, and our part in it became comparatively small till the work had made progress.

On Thursday, the 25th, the day proving favourable, the meeting was called in the Market Square, where an immense crowd assembled at half-past six. From the top of a stair Mr. W. C. Burns addressed upwards of 3000 from Ps. lxxi, 16, "I will go in the strength of the Lord God." The emotions of the audience were powerful, but for the most part silent,

* Mr. W. C. Burns found it impossible to leave a scene so interesting, and Mr. Lyon went to Dundee to supply his place.

though now and then there might be the utterance of feeling, and, in countenances beyond numbering, expressions of earnest and serious concern. Six young girls, from fourteen to sixteen years, two of them orphans, came next day bathed in tears, and seeking Christ. The scene was deeply affecting. This day (26th) many conversations were held by Mr. W. C. Burns in the session-house; by myself and my other son (on trial for licence) in the manse. Upon Sabbath, the 28th, the church was crowded, and with the unusual appearance of not a few females without bonnets, and men and children in week-day and working dresses. I preached from Heb. iv, 16. In the afternoon we met at three in the churchyard, where there assembled not fewer than 4000. The sermon by Mr. W. C. Burns was solid and impressive, from Rom. viii, 1. He finished about five o'clock; but after the blessing was pronounced, about a third part either remained or soon returned, of various ages, but especially young, which led to various questionings, at first, and then remarks, and appeals frequently repeated, which led to great meltings of heart in many, and, in a few cases, to considerable agitation; so much so, that my son and I continued to address the hearers in various ways, and to sing and pray over and over again, the people still unwilling to depart. Four of our pious men, two of whom were elders, were called to pray at intervals, which they did in a most appropriate and affecting manner. Even at half-past eight it was with difficulty we got to a close, proposing to have a meeting next morning at seven in the church. A great many still pressed around as we left the churchyard for the manse, and several remained till eleven or twelve o'clock. Next morning I went to the church at seven, after calling on an aged woman on the way, whose cries of distress arrested me. Even at that early hour there were from two to three hundred met in solemn silence, joining with me in prayer and praise, and listening to a short exposition of Song, ii, 10—14. Through the whole day conversations were held in the manse, and in the vestry and session-house. In the evening the bell rung at half-past six. The church being before that filled, and as great a number pressing forward, it was found necessary to adjourn to the Market Square. Mr. Somerville of Anderston addressed a very large assembly of most attentive hearers, from John, xvi, 14. At the close I was called to see three or four very affecting cases of mental distress, and there was still a desire to get more of the word and prayer. There was an adjournment to the church, where at first, as I understand (for I was engaged as above stated), there was considerable excitement, but which subsided into solemn and deep emotion, while Mr. W. C. Burns and Mr. Somerville addressed the people, and joined in prayer and praise. Next day at eleven *a.m.* Mr Somerville again addressed a full congregation in the church.

Ever since the date to which I have brought this imperfect narrative, with the exception of one evening, we have had meetings every evening for prayer, for the most part along with preaching of the Word. On the evening referred to (the 6th August), there was held a meeting in the Relief church, which, was crowded by various classes, the work expressly approved of by the ministers present, Mr. W. Anderson of Glasgow, and Mr. Banks of Paisley. From the first the people of the Relief congregation seemed interested in the work equally with our own people, and there appears to this day to be much of the spirit or love diffused among us. The state of society is completely changed. Politics are quite over with us. Religion is the only topic of interest. They who passed each other before, are now seen shaking hands, and conversing about the all-engrossing subject. The influence is so generally diffused, that a stranger going at hazard into any house would find himself in the midst of it.

The awakening in the newly-erected parish of Banton has of late become most intensely interesting. At a prayer meeting in the school there, the whole present, above one hundred men and women, not a few of them hardened miners and colliers, were melted. Every night since this day week there have been meetings in the church of Banton, and many earnest enquirers. The missionary, Mr. Lyon, whose labours have been for upwards of a year greatly blessed, has been aided, as I have been, by many excellent friends in the ministry, and the work goes on there in a manner fully as surprising as here. I am under obligations to my brethren for their ready and efficient services. I may just mention Mr. Duncan of Glasgow, Mr. Macnaughtan of Paisley, Mr. Moody of Edinburgh, Mr. M'Donald of Urquhart, and Mr. Jamieson Willis, as having been longest with us, and given valuable assistance; with Mr. Salmon, our former teacher.

We are tried by the intrusion among us of teachers who are likely to sow divisions, some of them, no doubt, much safer in doctrine than others. Strangers also who come among us, from good motives, are in danger of injuring our converts by over-kindness, and bringing them too much into notice. Enemies are waiting for occasion of triumph; and professors of religion, of a cold description, are doubting and waiting a long time ere they trust that any good is doing. Meantime the work proceeds most certainly; and from day to day there are additions to the "Church of such as shall be saved." The sermons preached are none of them eccentric or imaginative, but sound and scriptural; and there is not, as formerly, a tendency to compare the merits of preachers, but a hearing in earnest, and for life and death.

The waiting on of young and older people at the close of each meeting, and the anxious asking of so many "what to do"—the lively singing of the praises of God, which every visitor remarks—the complete desuetude of swearing and foolish talking in our streets—the order and solemnity at all hours pervading ; the song of praise and prayer almost in every house—the cessation of the tumults of the people—the consignment to the flames of volumes of infidelity and impurity*—the coming together for Divine worship and heavenly teaching of such a multitude of our population day after day—the large catalogue of new intending communicants giving in their names, and conversing in the most interesting manner on the most important subjects—not a few of the old, careless sinners, and other frozen formalists, awakened, and made alive to God—the conversion of several poor colliers,† who have come to me, and given the most satisfactory account of their change of mind and heart, are truly wonderful proofs of a most surprising and delightful revival.

The case of D. S., collier, may be mentioned as interesting. He had for sometime been thoughtful, and had given up entirely taking any intoxicating liquor, and might be characterised as one of the more hopeful description. Since the present awakening, he was deeply convinced of his sin and misery, and for a month was deeply exercised and spending much time in secret prayer and reading the Scriptures. On the evening of the 21st August, he had a meeting with several of his praying companions, and spent the night in prayer, praise, and converse. He appears to have obtained peace during that night, and came home to his house in a very happy state of mind. After taking two hours' rest, he worshipped with his family, and proceeded to his work. Being the foreman, it was his lot to descend first into the pit, which he did with unusual alacrity and with prayer. On reaching the bottom, the air instantly exploded, and in a moment he was ushered into eternity! How soothing and cheering the thought that he has escaped the everlasting burnings, and has passed literally through the fire to the regions of glory!

But the bounds of this communication will not permit enlargement. The work I consider as ongoing and increasing. The limits of Satan's domains here are diminishing daily. The account not a few give of their conversion is, that they could not think of being left a prey when others were making their escape. There is thus a provision made for the increase of the

---

* W. S. in presence of an elder and several witnesses with his own hand took down some books of this description, and put them in the fire.

† A. B., T. A., J. S., W. P., and A. M., colliers, all joined at the communion, after giving very satisfactory accounts of their conversion.

kingdom of Christ by a kind of laudable jealousy—a pressing in ere the door be shut.

I have been engaged, and still continue to be engaged, in conversing with new communicants; and never before now have I had such pleasant work in listening to, and marking down, the accounts which the youngest to the oldest give of the state of their minds. While some, who seem to be savingly impressed, have given a somewhat *figurative* account of their feeling, yet, in by far the greater number of instances, they give most Scriptural and intelligible accounts of their convictions, and of the grounds on which they rest their peace. Their experiences are evidently so various, as not to be in any degree copies of each other. Yet they all end in building upon the sure foundation, Christ in the promise, and Christ formed in them. The question naturally occurs, and has been put, "Is there any thing peculiar in the subjects and mode of address of the sermons which have been so remarkably successful?" I answer, that upon a groundwork of solid, clear, and simply expressed views of divine truth, there was a great measure of affectionate, earnest pleading, rich exhibition of the fulness and freeness of the Gospel, eminently calculated to convey to the hearers the conviction and feeling of the sincerity of the preacher, and of the rich grace of the Lord Jesus. It has also been a matter of general remark, that there is an unction and deep solemnity in the *prayers* of the preacher who has been honoured to begin this work, and which, perhaps, even more than the sermons, have made way to the heart. We have had much precious truth presented to us by my much beloved brethren, to whom it must be gratifying to be assured, that in conversations with my people, there have been references, I may say, to each of their discourses, as having been profitable, as well as acceptable; and that having been so well supported by their co-operation, and the Presbyterial notice taken of the subject, we cherish the pleasing hope, that, under the special and continuing blessing of the great Head of the Church, this will prove not only a genuine, but an extensive and a permanent revival—the only means of arresting our downward course, and effecting that blessed consummation, which the diffusion of merely intellectual knowledge will never accomplish.

WILLIAM BURNS,
Minister of Kilsyth.

Manse, Kilsyth, Sept. 16, 1839.

N. B.—On the 20th January this year, there was held a meeting of a newly-organised Missionary Society, addressed by myself, Mr. Lyon, Mr. W. C. Burns, and Mr. John Adam, student in divinity, which forms an era in this parish. A good many who had taken no interest formerly in religious concerns, began from this date to attend meetings, and to give weekly offerings to the collection; and this is referred to by not a few as a time of refreshing.

Account of the Communion 22nd September, 1839.

About three weeks after this remarkable work commenced, it was considered most desirable and obligatory to have *another* communion season. The Session met for special prayer for direction as to the matter, and afterward as to the *time* most suitable.

The number of new communicants amounts to nearly ninety. A few who spoke on the subject seem to have had scruples, and did not come forward. With the exception of a very few, the account given of their views and spiritual condition has been very pleasing and satisfying. They vary in regard to age from twelve to three score and ten; a good many are from fifteen to eighteen years of age. The work of examining has been of a different character from that of former years, wherein " *we have seen evil.*" No doubt the systematic knowledge of not a few of them is deficient, and much pains must be taken by themselves and by us in this matter. I have urged on the young converts especially a very careful study of the Shorter Catechism, and the earnest, close, and prayerful study of the Scriptures. We solicit the prayers of Christian friends and ministers, that we may have the great joy of seeing our children " walking in the truth," and *established with grace.*

The number of communicants would doubtless have been greater had we deferred the communion for a few weeks, as the Banton revival is not so far advanced as to have furnished a large addition.*

A great concourse of people, including not a few genuine friends of the Lord Jesus, assembled to our communion. It is thought that not fewer than from twelve to fifteen thousand were *in and about* the town of Kilsyth upon the Lord's day; at the Tent the number is estimated at about ten or twelve thousand. The day was uncommonly favourable; and indeed during the whole interesting season external circumstances were most propitious, and having been made the matter of special prayer, the answer should be marked and remembered.

On the Fast day (Thursday) public worship began at the usual hour, the minister commencing with praise and prayer, and reading Psalms cxxvi and cxxx. The Rev. C. J. Brown of Edinburgh preached from Rom. vii, 9, " I was alive without the law once," &c. The Rev. Dr. Malan of Geneva preached in the afternoon from John, xiv, 29, " Peace I leave with you," &c. Mr. Macnaughtan of Paisley in the evening from Isa. xlii, 3, " A bruised reed shall he not break," &c. He preached also at Banton, and Mr. Cunningham of Edinburgh from the words in Rom. v, 8, " God *commendeth his love* to us." Friday evening the Rev. Mr. Middleton of Strathmiglo preached from Jer. viii, 22, " Is there no balm in Gilead, is there no physician there?" Saturday Mr. W. C. Burns preached in the tent to a large assembly from Rom. x, 4, " Christ is the end of the law," &c. In the evening Mr. Somerville of Anderston preached to a crowded audience from John xvi, on the work of the Spirit. This was a remarkable night of prayer, secret and social; probably there was not an hour or watch of the night altogether silent. The beds were not much occupied: many, like the Psalmist, prevented the dawning of the morning. The morning bell rung at nine o'clock, and worship began at fully twenty minutes to ten, both in church and at the tent. The action sermon was from John, vi, 35, " I am the bread of life," &c. Mr. Brown of Edinburgh fenced the tables. Mr. Rose of Glasgow preached in the Tent and fenced the tables.

The first table, as usual, contained about 100; but to prevent confusion and undue protraction of the services, arising from so unusual a num-

* The friends of the good cause are requested to remember *that* very interesting new parish, and to assist us with the means of having our very useful missionary ordained as soon as possible. It would be truly interesting to have, in the course of a few months, a communion season *there for the first time.* Subscriptions in aid of Banton will be received by myself and by Mr. Robert Moody, Writer, Glasgow.

ber of communicants, the second was composed of those already seated in the body of the church ; after this the third was composed of those in the usual bounds, with a few seats additional, and the remainder were served in the usual tables, so that the great accession was not felt as any obstruction to order or comfort. The ministers were at full liberty to address the communicants without the constant urgency of studied brevity. There were eight services as follows :— The Minister, 1st; Mr Martin of Bathgate, 2nd ; Mr. Dempster of Denny, 3rd ; Mr. Brown, 4th ; Mr. Somerville, 5th ; Mr. Rose, 6th ; Mr. Duncan, Kirkintilloch, 7th; and Dr. Dewar, 8th.

Mr. Rose preached in the evening from Isaiah, xlii, 3. All over by nine, without interval. In the tent, after Mr. Rose, Mr. W. C. Burns, Mr. Middleton, Mr. Somerville, and Dr. Dewar preached. Mr. W. C. Burns preached again, by moonlight, to a great assembly, from " The mountains may depart," &c. All was most orderly and decorous, and in many cases there were symptoms of deep emotion. We have heard of several well authenticated cases of persons who came with levity of mind and went away deeply impressed; and of one or two who *could not get away*, but remained over Monday. Besides the vast crowd at the tent, Messrs. Martin, Dempster, Brown, and Harper (of Bannockburn) severally addressed groups of people near the church, waiting for entrance to the tables.* After public service, a great number of the godly strangers, and of our younger members, and of persons concerned about salvation, remained. The younger ministers present continued in exhortation, prayer, and psalms successively, for a considerable time in a most solemn affectionate manner, feeling unusual enlargement in their own spirits, with much of the felt gracious presence of God.

On Monday, at a quarter past eleven, probably from two to three thousand assembled around the tent.† Dr. Dewar preached from John, xvi, 5, " He (the Spirit of truth) will convince the world of sin," &c. Mr. W. C. Burns preached from Ezek. xxxvi, 23—26, " A new heart will I give you," &c. The hour of five struck ere all was over, and very few withdrew previously. The sensation was deep and solemn. In the evening Mr. Brown preached in the church from " What do ye more than others ?" Similar exercises were engaged in also on the Monday night as on Sabbath night: which the ungodly jeer at, the formal wonder at and censure, and which many good Christians would at first pronounce rather carrying it too far. But the fact is, that this is a spring-tide, a very uncommon season, in which a rigid adherence to the rules of ordinary times must not be applied. We have been drawing up a large draught, and the nets cannot be kept and laid by so orderly and silently as usual.

This precious season of communion is now over and gone, but the remembrance is sweet. Having been preceded, accompanied, and followed by a very unusual copiousness of prayer, the showers in answer have been very copious and refreshing. We are daily hearing of good done to strangers, who came Zaccheus-like to see what it was, who have been pierced in heart and have gone away new men. Our own people of Christian spirit have been greatly enlivened and strengthened, and some very hopeful cases of apparently real beginnings of new life have been brought to our knowledge. I feel grateful to the God of grace and God of order in the churches, that there has been such a con-

* The communion proceeded in the ordinary way in the Relief church, with the assistance of Mr. Frew from St. Ninians

† Many ministers were present that day. Besides those already mentioned we noticed Mr. Laurie of Gargunnock, Mr. Leitch, Stirling, Mr. Hetherington of Torphichen, Mr. Cochran, Cumbernauld, Mr. J. Willis, Mr. Bonar, & Mr. Morison of Larbert, and Mr. Jeffrey, Paisley. Mr. Lee of Campsie was present upon Saturday, and on the Sabbath Mr. Forman of Kirkintilloch and Mr. Cochran. Many excellent elders also were present assisting us, as Mr. R. Brown, Fairley Dr. Russell, Edinburgh, Mr. R. Moody, Mr. H. Knox, Mr. John Robertson, Mr. Ilay Burns, Mr. Penney, Glasgow, Mr Simpson, Port Glasgow, Mr. M'Donald, Cochno, Bailie Shaw, Rutherglen, and Bailie M'Kenzie, Inverness.

currence of what is true, *venerable*, pure, just, lovely, and of good report, and that little indeed has escaped from any of us which can justly cause regret. We are anxious (we trust we have a good conscience) that nothing should be done against, but every thing *for* the truth, that God in all things may be glorified through Jesus Christ. The solemn appearance of the communion tables, and the delightful manner in which they were exhorted—the presence of not a few unusually *young* disciples at the tables—the seriousness of aspect in all, and the softening and melting look of others, made upon every rightly disposed witness a very delightful impression. May the Lord give abundant increase.

For ninety years, doubtless, there has not been in this parish such a season of prayer and holy communings and conferences—nor at any period such a number of precious sermons delivered: the spiritual awakening and the genuine conversions at this time are not few, and it is hoped will come forth to victory. But the annals of eternity only will divulge the whole! The *enemy*, the Devil, has been also among us, and is doubtless busy *now*—more so than at the time of this dispensation. We are not ignorant of his devices.

Yet upon the whole, there is much cause indeed to give God the glory for what he hath wrought. That he hath been the chief worker is most undoubted, for "the Son of God was manifested to destroy the works of the Devil," and his works have been much damaged and brought down among us. The public houses, the coalpits,* the harvest reaping fields, the weaving loom-steads, the recesses of our glens, and the sequestered haughs around, all may be called to witness, that there is a mighty change in this place for the better.

The wicked scoff—nay, some we hear around us, or passing by, have brought upon themselves the great guilt of speaking evil of this work. We pray for them. "They know not what they do!" Some decent professors and moral people, are opposed to this whole work, and say, "If it continue, it may do good," but they do nothing to make it continue, and others throw cold water upon it. It is strange, that when sermons seem to make no impression, these persons should feel no anxiety about the permanency of the good expected—but when there is really appearance of good impressions, their doubt should be expressed about the duration of the good promised. Shall we be satisfied that we preach, and are heard, and no one showing any concern, but just sitting, and it may be, sleeping out the hours, and returning home as they came? Surely, surely evena degree, yea, a great deal of enthusiasm, is better than death-like insensibility.

Such godly fear has come upon the people, that scarcely a single instance of intoxication, or any approach to it, has been observed in the whole multitude assembled, whereas formerly the prevalence of this and the quarrels it engendered brought dishonour on tent-preaching, and in fact extinguished it.

Special instances of good done are naturally called for. Many memorable cases can be produced. Selection is difficult. A woman from Airdrie was observed by a few around her to be much impressed while Mr. W. C. Burns preached. She at length left the field and retired for prayer. After a little she was followed by some praying people, who conversed with her. She seems to have undergone a complete change, and went away in a composed frame. A young gentleman from Glasgow, with whom I and Mr. Brown conversed, who had come with some indefinite notion of good or of being pleased, went home a new man in

* A coal master here bears witness, that the colliers who were formerly drunk ten days in the month, ar now sober, and that instead of swearing, they have prayer-meetings below ground, and are orderly. And why should colliers not be numbered among saints, and be kings and priests to God? Pious colliers and miners, what a treasure!

Christ Jesus. I know several cases of whole houses being really converted. Mrs. H. has been converted in a very wonderful way. She had been a very passionate regardless character, who with her husband and family spent the Sabbath day in drinking, and other tainted enormities; two pious women, unknown to each other, had called upon her, telling her that they could get no rest till they came to warn her of her sin and danger. The poor woman thought with herself, if these two are so concerned about me that they cannot get rest, what should be my concernment about myself. She attended a prayer meeting, came home at midnight, and roused her family to tell them of her change of mind. There seems a very remarkable work of grace with the husband, and other branches of the family.

A. B., collier, aged fifty, a month ago, was upon the road side on the way from the church in great agony of mind when I passed homewards. I at first thought he had been *in drink :* but it turned out that he had Hannah-like been pouring out his heart before the Lord, having got a sight of his sinfulness; he went to his bible and prayed; got heartening, as he expressed it, from the thought that had come to him, ' Shall I be a castaway?' Enabled to lay hold on Christ as the Ransomer, and as having paid the debt, he said, " Come life, come death, I will depend on his merits and mercies:" resolving to be with Christ henceforward. On receiving his token, he said, " I used to run from you, but am now happy to meet. I served Satan fifty years: I am now the Lord's." His two companions, J. S. and T. A., gave very satisfactory accounts of their change of heart, and are also communicants. The accounts of other cases more detached and interesting must be deferred.

I add a very few words in the way of inference.

1st, Prayer united, as well as secret, for the bestowal of the Spirit's influence, is most important, and will sooner or later be heard.

2ndly, *Extra* means should be used to bring those *without the pale* of any church to hear the Gospel. The preaching the former summer in the church-yard once and again, and the late frequent addresses in the market and field, have most certainly brought the word near to many who might have remained to their dying day without hearing it. Assuredly these means must be used, otherwise our newly provided churches will remain unoccupied, and in a great degree useless.

3rd, There is a close connection betwixt *Missionary* work and revivals. Our newly organized Missionary Society, in January this year, has been marked by several people as an era. No church can be in a lively state when nothing is done for the heathen.

4th, The social nature of man is an important element in his constitution, and exerts a powerful influence on the state of the church and of the world. There are those who view the weavers' shops as objects of unmingled aversion, as hotbeds of anarchy; but when a good influence is made to bear upon the minds of the operatives the facilities for *good* are proportional to those for evil—the reviving interest spreads much quicker than in a rural district. Let every minister of the Gospel, and every Christian patriot keep this steadily in view, and ply the workshops with every good and generous influence. Never let us cease in good times and bad, to essay to do good, in the morning sowing seed, and in the evening withholding not our hand: thus are we to sow beside all waters. God give the increase!

W. B.

Kilsyth, 30th September, 1839.